PEEPSHOW COLLECTIVE

Luke Best
Jenny Bowers
Miles Donovan
Chrissie Macdonald
Pete Mellor
Marie O'Connor
Andrew Rae
Elliot Thoburn
Lucy Vigrass
Spencer Wilson

Peepshow Collective
Published by:
Index Book, S.L.
Consell de Cent 160 local 3
08015 Barcelona
Spain
T: +34 934 545 547
F: +34 934 548 438
ib@indexbook.com
www.indexbook.com

Copyright 2012
© Index Book, S.L.

Publisher:
Sylvie Estrada

Design:
Studio EMMI
www.emmi.co.uk

ISBN: 978-84-15308-12-6

CONTENTS

FOREWORDS
Alex Bec

The best things happen because they have to. The first shoes were probably invented because cavemen were hurting their feet on the way to the shops. The wheel, because it was taking ages to get to the shops; and bags, because there was too much to put on the wheel on the way back from the shops. My examples may be glib, but there is little doubt that real, genuine challenges spawn beautiful solutions.

And what has this got to do with Peepshow Collective? Loads. Peepshow only exists because of a challenge presented to a group of talented and motivated individuals taking their first steps out of art college. They did so at the turn of the century, when the internet and all of the networking opportunities it brought with it were comparably inconspicuous. No blogs. No Facebook. No Twitter. No guarantee that someone would stumble across your work on a regular online inspiration scour and hand you a much-needed bit of work. So, what better way of making sure your mates were all as well represented at client meetings as you were? Bring everyone's work with you, so that even if you weren't right for the job, the commission stayed in the family. A simple thought in the effortlessly linked-up world of today, but one that in 2000 took an ample amount of naive sharpness.

The results that followed were far from unexpected. Work flowed in, pencils were sharpened, studios were rented, reputations were built, and now we look at one of the most impressive bodies of work ever to be produced under the broad banner of 'illustration'. Anyhow, I digress; I'm supposed to be talking about what I know about Peepshow. Not what everyone knows about Peepshow – that their work is of a standard envied by every single aspiring image-maker.

The real magic goes far deeper than any of the reams of editorials, album covers, adverts or music videos that represent them. What makes Peepshow special is something that's been with them from day one – an unwavering generosity, spirit and respect for each other and their peers. In the true meaning of the term 'collective', Peepshow have huddled together to make a cooperative enterprise, but more importantly a living, breathing and caring family intent on making ends meet doing what they loved.

Like so many before and after me, I made the graduate pilgrimage from university to London armed with a degree in the creative arts, and very little idea of exactly what I was going to do with it. I'd introduced myself to Peepshow a couple of years before through some university projects, as well as some embarrassing fan-boy level visits to their stalls at the V&A village fete. Somehow it turned out that they were looking for some help in the studio, and that I was looking for some help filling my days and so I became the first, and subsequently only, person ever to work for them. They made what could have been a taxing time of moving to London complete bliss. The freedom to come in as many days as I could fit in around personal work, the responsibility to lead exciting projects with people I looked up to, and more importantly advice and respite whenever needed. I realised very quickly that I was in the company of something remarkable and am eternally grateful for the stepping stone they laid for me to find my feet in the big smoke.

Since leaving to pursue my own projects, my ears have been finely tuned to the sound of numerous 'collectives' springing out of illustration courses all over the world. Each have their own missions and intentions, but none ever seem quite as plainly honest and necessary as Peepshow's were back in 2000. For that reason their success comes as no surprise and, if necessity truly is the mother of invention, then Peepshow are without doubt the forefathers of the illustration collective.

What I don't know is how, to this day, they continue to produce work of such a tirelessly high standard, but what I do know is that one way or another, they always will.

Alex Bec
Director, It's Nice That

Margaret Huber

The Brighton element of Peepshow were among the first group of students I interviewed when I started teaching at Brighton. As course leader for the BA Illustration, I was able to watch the students develop over their three years there, working with some as their personal tutor, participating in assessments and offering support as needed.

The first memory I have of them as a group was when they were in Level One. Gary Powell came into my office and said that I might want to come and see what some of his students were doing. I sat in on a group presentation and they were all doing extraordinary things, going way beyond what had been asked of them. I remember feeling excited about seeing work that was so ambitious and full of promise.

As course leader, my favourite part of the job was talking to students in the studio. I sometimes think that after teaching for over 25 years my memory of students is bound to have developed a few holes, but with this group I can recall particular conversations and specific work they produced. I can remember Luke Best, sitting at his desk, painting a series of images for his Othello project on the sides of empty crisp boxes. He had an old spoon that he used for mixing colours. It had lots of layers of acrylic paint and he had drawn a little face on it. I wanted it, but as his personal tutor thought it might look bad if I started buying work from him. When he finished the course I asked him about the spoon and whether he might consider selling it, but he said he had thrown it away.

Peepshow have always been great ambassadors for the Brighton Illustration programme: enthusiastic, talented and enterprising. Being a part of their transition from students to professionals, and seeing all they have accomplished since, has been a great pleasure.

A simple job offer to work on Expo with Graham in the early days of their careers has led to a long and continued friendship with the group, which is something I treasure – perhaps even more than I would have treasured the spoon.

Margaret Huber
Course Leader
MA Sequential Design/Illustration
MA Arts and Design by Independent Project
University of Brighton

Graham Rawle

I first met the Peepers in 1999, a year before they formed as a group. I'd been invited to create a 4,000 square foot supermarket installation for Expo 2000 in Hanover. I needed helpers and Margaret suggested some Brighton graduates she'd kept in touch with who she thought would be good. I started out working with Lucy and Miles, and soon others came on board to help out: Chrissie, Andrew, 'Little' Graham Carter, Jenny and Lenny, Luke and Chris Joscelyne – along with others from outside the group.

For six months, most of us spent all day every day working together. We had great fun, but the hours were long, the diet was poor and the conditions were sometimes less than uplifting. Because the budget was so small, for the most part people weren't even getting paid. I assured them that, like the physical exhaustion they were experiencing, this could be extremely character building. I also encouraged them to think of hot glue gun burns as the battle-scars of creative endeavour. Margaret was both surprised and grateful that nobody murdered me for what I put them through. I had to agree. The team were incredibly loyal to me and not being murdered was an unexpected bonus.

The team were skilled and clever, but I think what impressed me most was their spirit – the way they set about every task with such enthusiasm, seeing each aspect of the work as an opportunity to come up with something funny and interesting. There was real collaboration. Everyone took pride in the work they were doing without feeling the need to claim ownership of it. (Peepshow have since proved to be adept at working as a group while retaining their individuality.) They had a finely tuned sense of humour that was very much akin to my own. We laughed a great deal at the things we were creating. I don't know if anyone else did; we were probably giddy from sleep depravation.

Looking back, I think we learned some valuable lessons: that driving while you're asleep is a bad idea, as is Domino's pizza, and that when searching through a bag of second-hand clothes, what at first may appear to be a fur coat might turn out to be a dead fox. There were other personal discoveries and insights too, which could be summed up thus: if you spend too much time scrabbling round in the dirt collecting rubbish, sooner or later you're going to come across a carrier bag full of human shit.

With Expo up and running and these life lessons fresh in their minds, the group went on to form the fabulous Peepshow Collective. In the intervening ten years, Margaret and I have watched them go from strength to strength as well as from studio to studio. Peepshow are like a family and they make us feel like we are part of that family, which is a great honour. We hope this means they're going to be looking after us in our old age.

Graham Rawle
Writer & Artist

The broom is a good example of the dubious ingenuity that prevailed during the Expo installation. Finding ourselves without a broom, Miles improvised with a dustpan brush, a length of 2 x 1 and a cable tie.

INTRO

There were seven of us, in the beginning. It was 2000, two years after we'd graduated from the University of Brighton. We were Graham Carter, Miles Donovan, Chris Joscelyne, Chrissie Macdonald, Andrew Rae, Lucy Vigrass and Spencer Wilson. We had degrees in illustration and no grand plan.

Our aim was to share costs; set up a website to showcase our individual work; draw strength in numbers. Because the site was based on a peephole, offering a glimpse into our illustration portfolios, we chose the name Peepshow and in September 2001 organised our first group exhibition, at the New Inn Yard Gallery in Shoreditch. At the same time, Angus Hyland's Pen & Mouse was published, featuring the work of Miles, Lucy and Spencer. We were already becoming known in the plural.

Yet Peepshow was never a fixed entity. In 2002, seven became 12 – as Luke Best, Jenny Bowers, James Lee Duffy, Marie O'Connor and Elliot Thoburn joined our ranks – and later dropped to nine, when Graham, Duffy and Chris left. Our final addition, Pete Mellor, who studied with us at Brighton, had already worked with us on joint projects. Slowly collaboration was creeping in alongside our individual work.

While our separate careers took their own twists and turns, there was a common thread we could keep coming back to. Peepshow provided continuity, and it also loosened us up: beyond illustration, we worked across moving image, set design, mixed media installation, fashion and textile design and art direction.

For the first four years, Peepshow was a group without a home – it was only in 2004 that we began to share a studio. That accelerated the process of cross-pollination, and helped us work on self-initiated activities which fed back into our commercial work. We set up stall at the V&A Village Fete three years' running; created an animation for Onedotzero at the Hayward Gallery; designed the title sequence for the Culture Show. And, more recently, we breathed life into the ICA's Heavy Pencil event, bringing it to Shoreditch with Heavy Pencil East and to Somerset House's Pick Me Up exhibition.

Looking back, it all coalesces into a neat timeline, but the grand plan was never there. That's why we haven't grouped this book into distinct sections, either chronological or thematic. We've never worked that way. Splitting our work into categories would have imposed a false sense of order onto a process that is more often messy than planned.

This book reveals what we do, in all that messiness – the different disciplines, approaches, visual languages and collaborations that make us Peepshow. It's not intended as a 'How To' of illustration; we don't believe there's one way of doing things, or one solution. In fact, we're still figuring it out.

From Start To Finish
Saatchi & Saatchi, London
2007

In the summer of 2007 we were asked to put together a show running the length of the windows of Saatchi & Saatchi advertising agency in London. Faced with such a large space and prominent location, we felt we wanted to create more of an impact than a simple print show. The decision was made to create a 3D installation spanning the length of the building – we just needed a concept. As a group, we had always enjoyed the problem-solving process and it was with this in mind we decided to illustrate the creation of an idea – taking this through a fantastical journey and arriving at the final artwork. Starting with a 'thought cloud', we followed our working process to fruition, taking in tea breaks, research completed, cogs whirring and colours selected. The narrative ended with resolved artwork tumbling from hand-made printers to fill the final window.

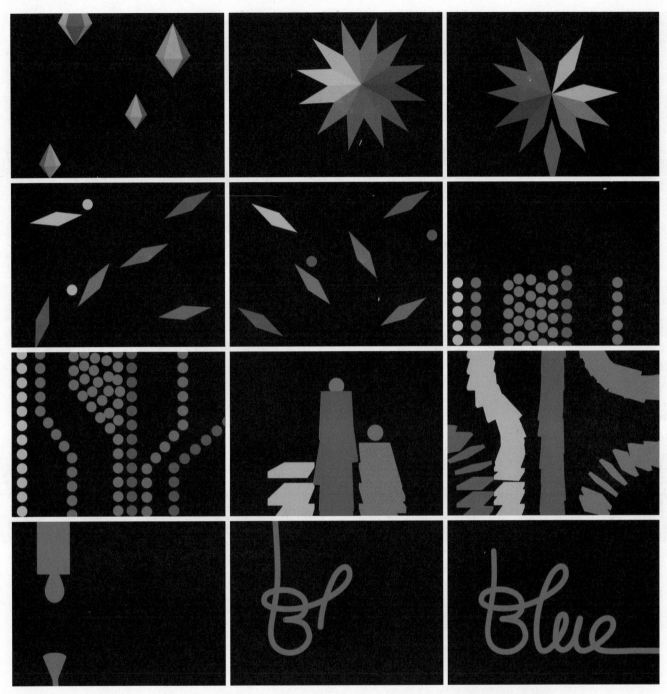

PETE MELLOR (Director)
Colour Picker (45")
Saatchi & Saatchi, London
2007
As part of the Peepshow 'problem
solving' we wanted to include some
sort of moving image element. This
animation provided the 'colour
selection' part of the process. The film
started by taking one of the physical
objects from the space – a shiny
cardboard diamond suspended over
the TV monitor – and taking it through
an energetic and colourful process
of elimination until the colour 'blue'
is settled upon.

LUCY VIGRASS
Pil Magazine
2000
This is my first published piece. I hand
delivered the artwork, as at the time
I didn't own a computer. I miss this
part of the job to a certain extent as
email and websites can make it easier
to be insular and less likely to build a
relationship with a client.

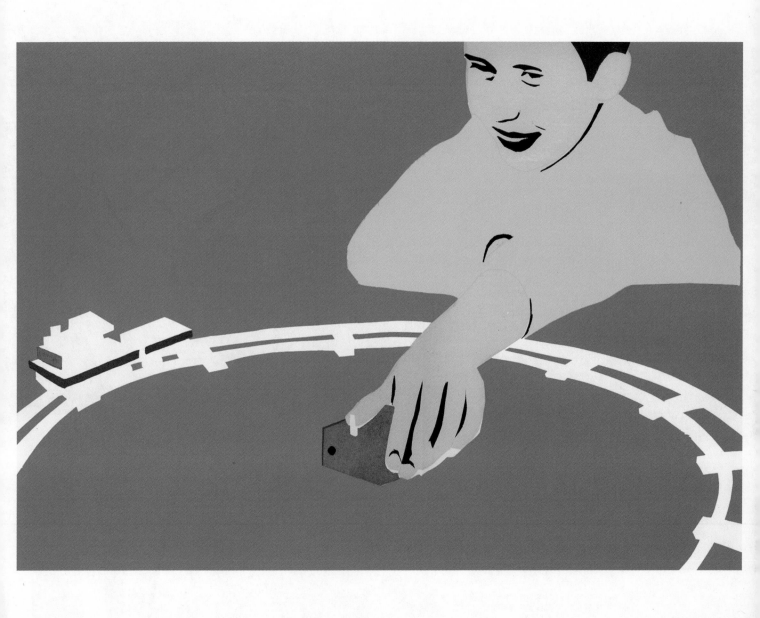

11

Clockwise from left:
LUCY VIGRASS
Cat On Chair
2000

Pointing
2000
Personal work created on my kitchen table by screen-printing with hand-cut paper stencils. This became the technique used in all my early editorial work and this technique still informs my work today with the use of bold shapes and flat colour. The palette from Pointing became my preferred colour range – and still is.

Boy
2000

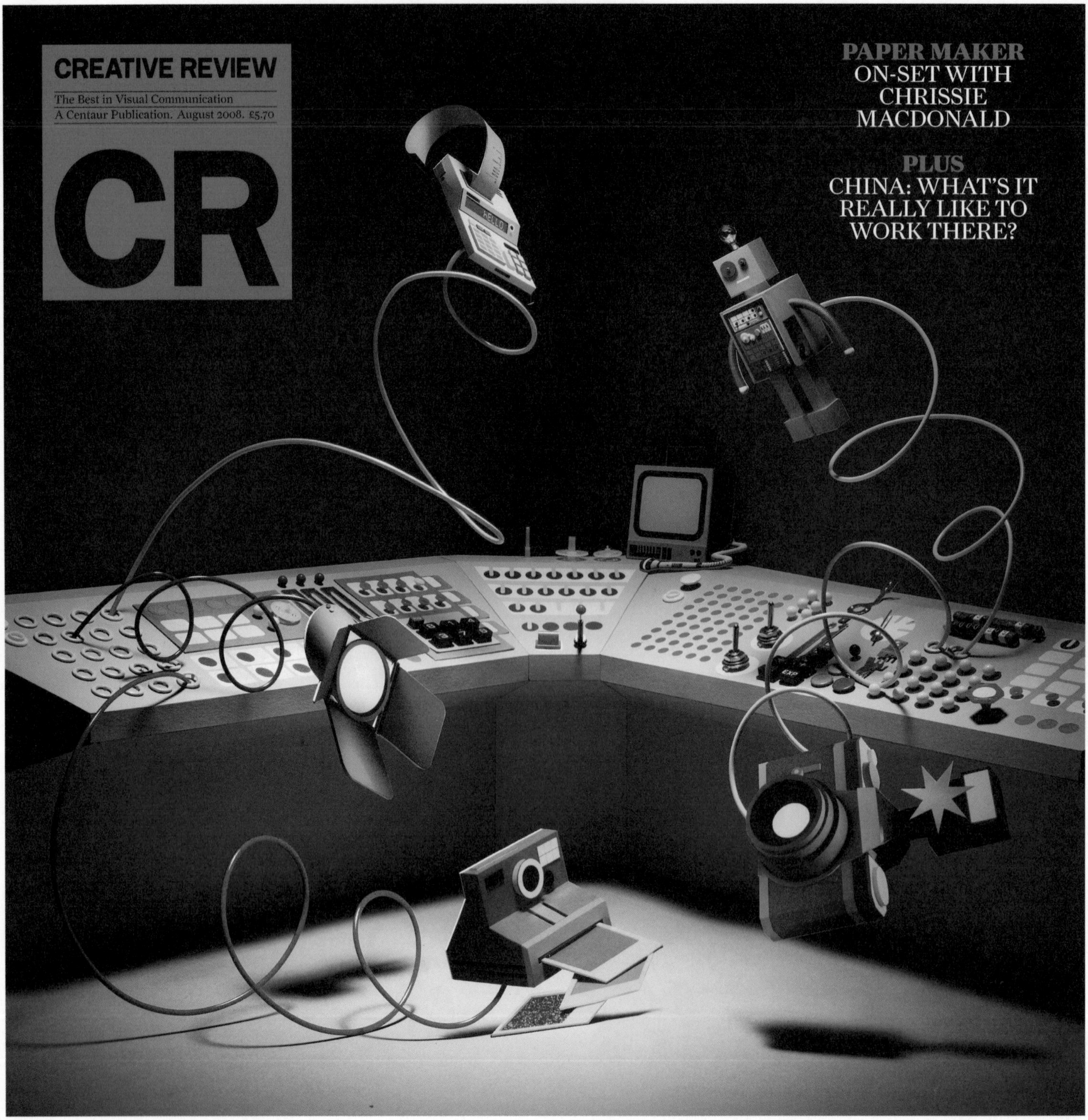

CREATIVE REVIEW

The Best in Visual Communication
A Centaur Publication. August 2008. £5.70

CR

PAPER MAKER
ON-SET WITH
CHRISSIE
MACDONALD

PLUS
CHINA: WHAT'S IT
REALLY LIKE TO
WORK THERE?

"I wanted to show a teacher being made fun of. It was denied by the censor. 'We must always respect our elders,' they said." Creative Johnny Tan on working in China

CHRISSIE MACDONALD
Creative Review
2008
Photography: John Short
This cover image was created to accompany an interview with me in the same issue. John and I selected various elements from previous commissions to spring from a control panel, suggesting an imaginary scenario of how the pieces were conceived.

CHRISSIE MACDONALD
Paper Shredder
Creative Review
2009
Photography: John Short
This was a very open brief as I was
simply asked to represent a range
of different paper stocks. I find more
enjoyment in designing pieces that
communicate an idea rather than
being purely decorative.

CHRISSIE MACDONALD
Bier
Creative Review
2009
Photography: John Short
As a follow-up to the shredder piece, this image was inspired by 1980s still-life compositions that often incorporate a selection of unlikely objects. The components are made from papers of the same name: Chocolate, China,

Ebony, Ivory, Lager, Pils and Marble. I originally planned to create the shadows from paper but this wasn't very effective so John cast them with real light instead. I really enjoy this part of the working process as the position of a light can completely transform the outcome of an image, which makes it a very collaborative process.

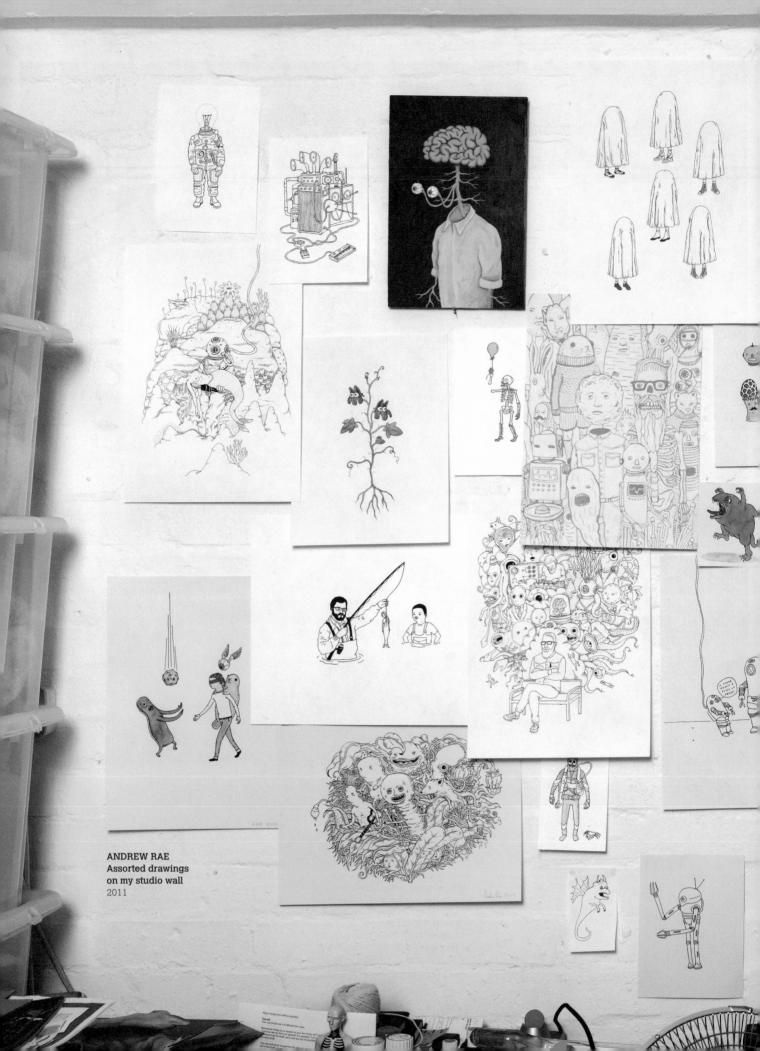

ANDREW RAE
Assorted drawings
on my studio wall
2011

DEVIL IN
THE DETAILS

BY ANDREW RAE AND JAMES CASEY

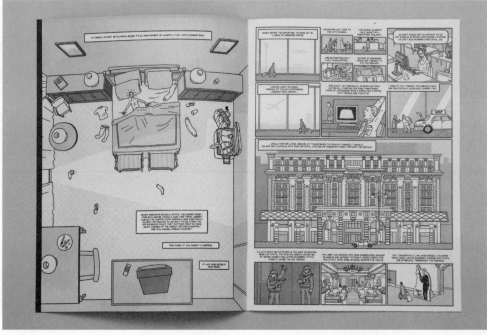

ANDREW RAE
Devil in the Details
Swallow Magazine
2010
Writer James Casey
This comic came free inserted within
Swallow Magazine, a pioneering
publication that redefines food
magazines. It tells the story of James
Casey losing his passport in Moscow
with inspiration from "The Master
and Margarita" by Mikhail Bulgakov.
It features full-frontal male nudity, an
evil human-sized cat and Laika the
Space Dog and it won a slice in the
D&AD awards 2011.

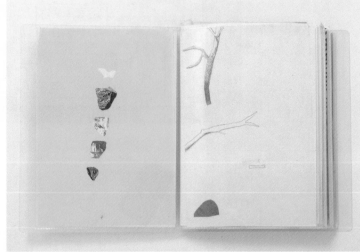

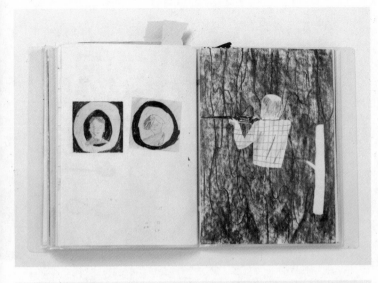

LUKE BEST
Folders
Selection from 2001–2011
offcuts/drawings/play

LUKE BEST
If I Could Do It All Again
It's a Long Way Back exhibition
KRETS Gallery, Malmo, Sweden
2011
160cm x 59cm

PETE MELLOR (Director)
2010: A Christmas Odyssey (45")
2010

At Peepshow I am surrounded by illustrations that don't move and I am often thinking about ways that they could. In this case, Spencer had recently produced a 3 colour letterpress planographic print called 'Space Cowboy'. I thought that I could make him move nicely and try out some ideas about mixing 2D and 3D animation. We have made several animations which we send out at Christmas and we thought this could be one of them. The interesting thing about this little personal project was that with a tight, self-imposed deadline (in between commercial projects), and no client to answer to, the original thumbnail sketches were translated very faithfully into the final animation.

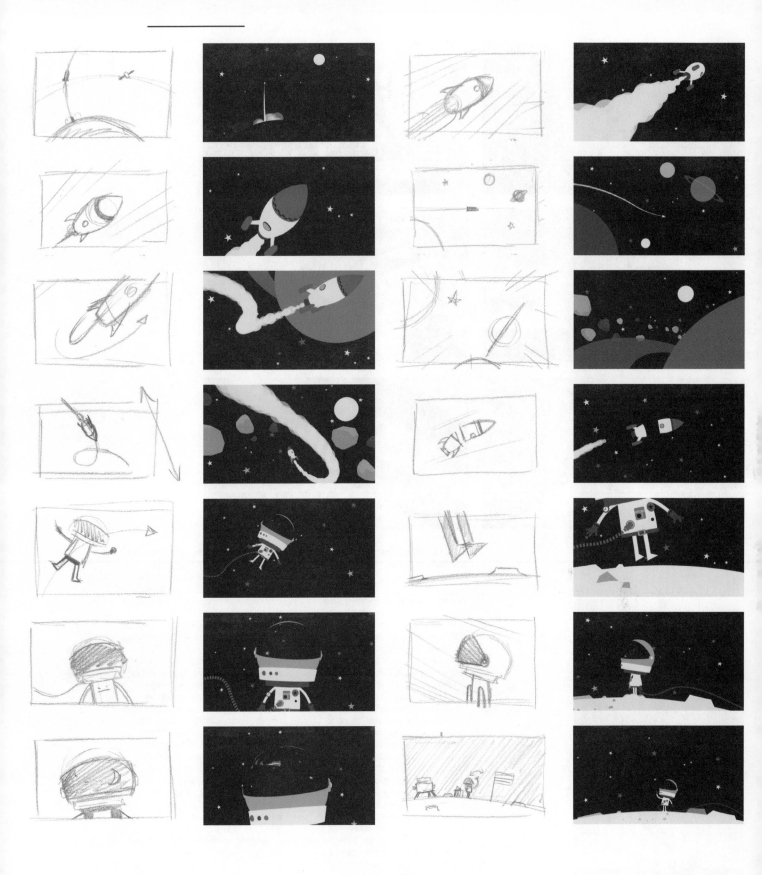

PETE MELLOR (Director)
The Culture Show (15")
BBC
2008
We may not work collectively on a single image very often but concepts and ideas for animations get better with input from different people. It is also a way of stepping outside of your own personal visual language and suggesting an idea without having to worry about how it would look. This means that a lot of the animation projects are ideas-led – with the style coming about as a means to communicate the idea in the most direct and appropriate way.

Almost all the animation commissions are discussed and considered by the group, but they are often taken to completion by a smaller team of one or two illustrators, an animator and a project manager or producer. The notable exceptions to this were our animation projects for Diesel and Nike. Both had quite open briefs, which allowed for ideas to come from everyone, and both had a collective approach to the art direction, with imagery coming from every member of Peepshow. The challenge then was to put all the ideas together so they would flow and to see how different illustrators' work sat next to one another.

The titles and stings for The Culture Show were a collaborative experience as, although there was a small team seeing the job through to the end, it required everyone to be involved at each of the different ideas stages. The job would not have been so successful without the input from the whole group, contributing solutions to problems, keeping the cultural references varied and not relying too heavily on cliches – although there's always room for a cliche when necessary. Lightbulbs feature heavily.

This collective approach to certain projects means that we can all continue to be surprised by the different directions our work can go in, keeping ourselves interested and our clients on their toes.

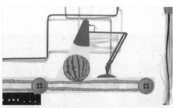

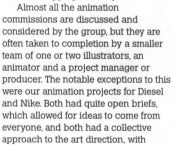

PEEPSHOW (Director)
Love The Ball (2'20")
Weiden + Kennedy/Nike
2006

PEEPSHOW (Director)
My Disco is Freezing (60")
KesselsKramer/Diesel
2004

This page:
Stylings for Sticky Problem, Sticky Solution

Opposite page:
PETE MELLOR (Director)
Decoding The Chatter –
Samsung (2'30")
Sticky Problem, Sticky Solution –
Unilever (2")
Tapping into A Global Ideas Bank
(2'20")
Sennep/Kantar
2009–2010
We created 3 films for Sennep's
re-design of the Kantar website.
Each film dealt with a particular
marketing case study so there
was a lot of factual copy to make
sense of. Each film needed to be
individual so art direction was
handled by different artists:
Luke Best; Spencer Wilson;
Lucy Vigrass and Miles Donovan.

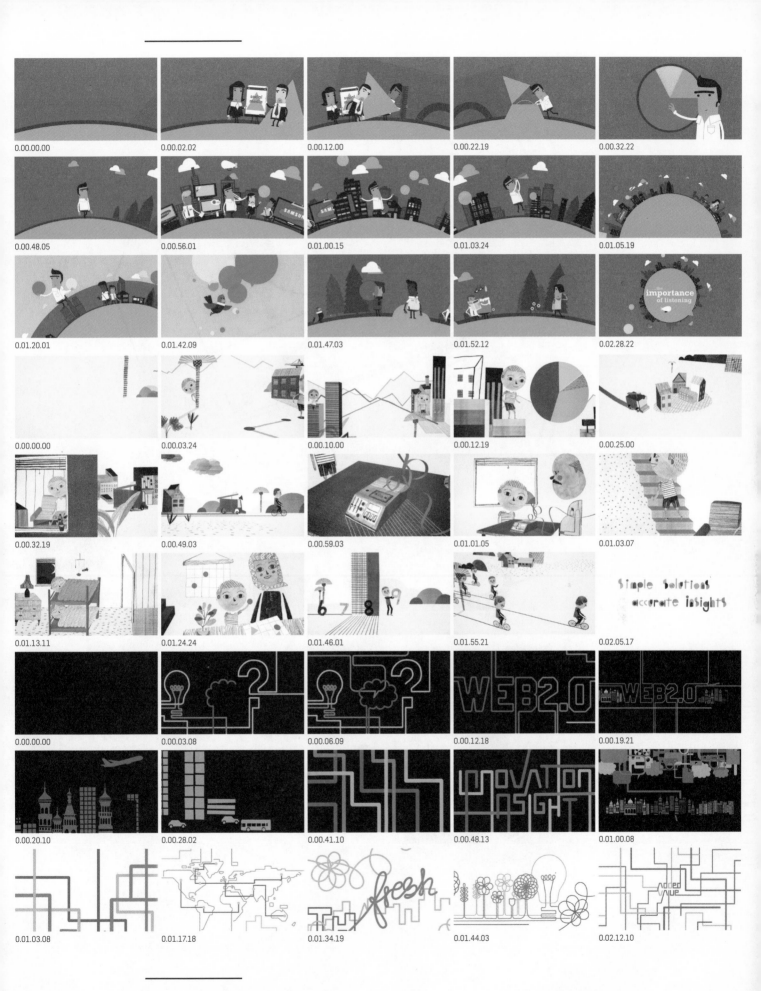

0.00.00.00　　0.00.02.02　　0.00.12.00　　0.00.22.19　　0.00.32.22

0.00.48.05　　0.00.56.01　　0.01.00.15　　0.01.03.24　　0.01.05.19

0.01.20.01　　0.01.42.09　　0.01.47.03　　0.01.52.12　　0.02.28.22

0.00.00.00　　0.00.03.24　　0.00.10.00　　0.00.12.19　　0.00.25.00

0.00.32.19　　0.00.49.03　　0.00.59.03　　0.01.01.05　　0.01.03.07

0.01.13.11　　0.01.24.24　　0.01.46.01　　0.01.55.21　　0.02.05.17

0.00.00.00　　0.00.03.08　　0.00.06.09　　0.00.12.18　　0.00.19.21

0.00.20.10　　0.00.28.02　　0.00.41.10　　0.00.48.13　　0.01.00.08

0.01.03.08　　0.01.17.18　　0.01.34.19　　0.01.44.03　　0.02.12.10

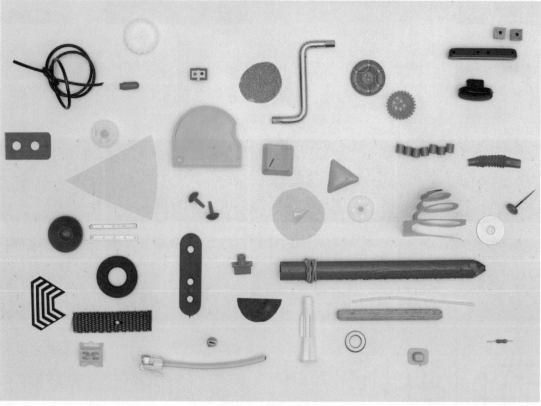

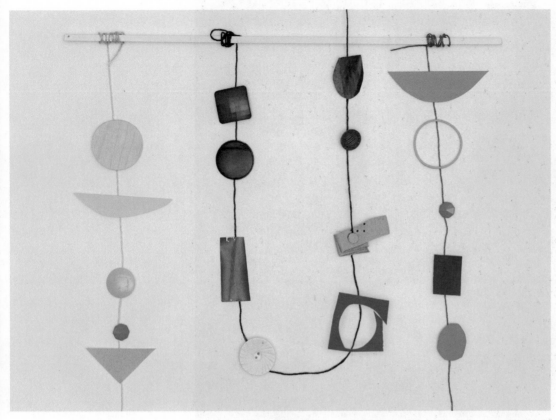

MARIE O'CONNOR
Creative Knowledge
Checkland Kindleysides
2009
Clockwise from top left:
Consumer Mindsets
Global Implementation
Viewpoints
Prototyping

MARIE O'CONNOR
Make_Shape
Norrköpings Konstmuseum, Sweden
2011
I was invited to create a workshop for
the event Does it fit? at Norrköpings
Konstmuseum. With my interactive
installation Make_Shape the public were
encouraged to test and try on objects
made of various materials – fabric, card,
wood and papier mache – creating
something between garments, jewellery
and sculpture.
    Some shapes were more obvious
in how they could be applied than
others. I was interested in how these
appendages could abstract, confine
or manipulate the body and limbs.
To overtake and dictate some kind
of stance or posture.

MILES DONOVAN
Creation 1
2009
Collage
42cm x 62cm

Creation 2
2009
Collage
42cm x 62cm
A personal project influenced by the collaged backgrounds to Jack Kirby's 1960s comic books, The Fantastic Four and Jimmy Olsen. These collages were created for the Peepshow exhibition Inbetween in the summer of 2009. My first work in a long, long time made completely unaided by a computer.

MILES DONOVAN
Field
2009
Collage
23cm x 36cm

Train
Swallow Magazine
2010
Collage

Next page:
Arctic
2009
Collage
42cm x 62cm

ELLIOT THOBURN
Seeing Double
Random House
2005

The Wrestling
Faber & Faber
2007

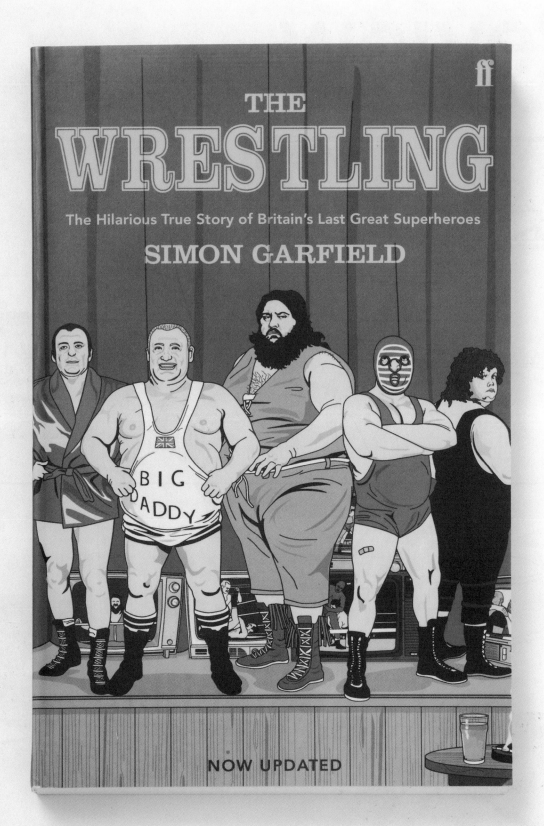

Review

ELLIOT THOBURN
Channel 4 Annual Report
Browns Design Ltd
2004

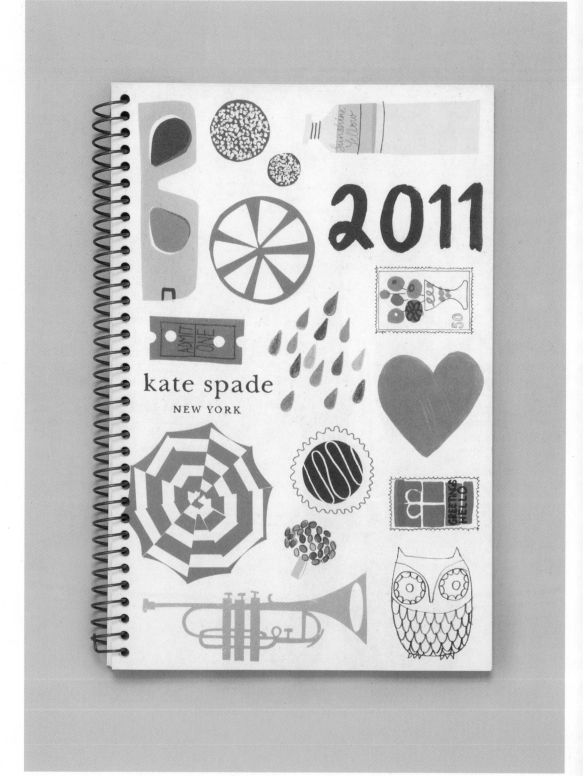

JENNY BOWERS
Kate Spade
Journal & Calendar 2011
2010
Working with the team at Kate Spade was great. They had a clear idea of the feel of the work they wanted and a single line of text for each calendar month, but were very open to the ideas I brought to each image. The relationship seemed reciprocal in terms of appreciation of certain references and enjoyment of colour. Overall it just seemed like a 'good fit'.

DECEMBER

spike the punch

SEPTEMBER

catch a double feature

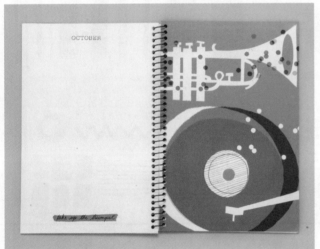

OCTOBER

take up the trumpet

JULY

send a postcard

MARCH

conquer the soufflé

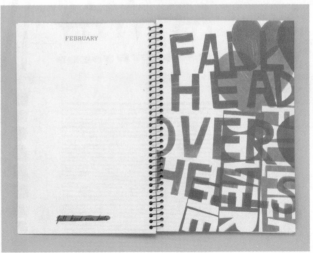

FEBRUARY

fall head over heels

JENNY BOWERS
Mark-making
Mark-making forms the mainstay of much of my work. I often start a job by producing pages of these simple marks and then playing with different combinations to form patterns and shapes. The simplicity of putting circles and lines together is always pleasing to me, making for a surprise and something unexpected every time. It is rare that I re-use the same mark, making new ones for each piece of work. I have reams of slightly different painted shapes.

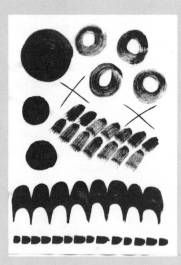

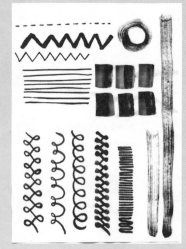

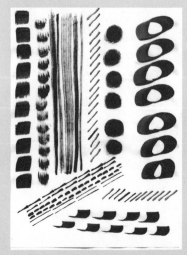

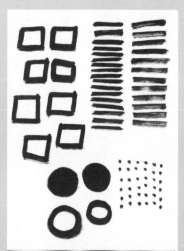

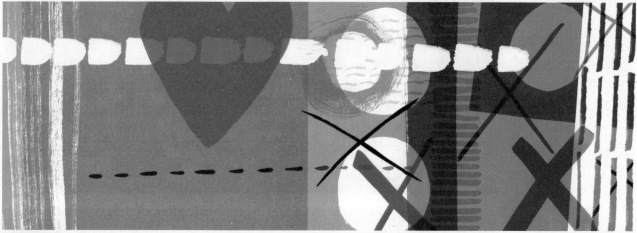

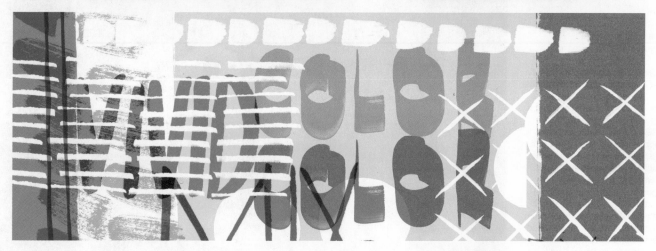

JENNY BOWERS
Vogue Nippon
Contents page illustrations
2011
Vogue Nippon allowed me great
freedom to create images to a very
open brief, with simple themes and
palettes drawn from fashion shoots
in each issue. A fun job.

Animal Mineral Veg Table
Scarlet Projects / V&A
2006

In 2006 Scarlet Projects invited us, for a third time, to create a stall for the annual designer Village Fete hosted by the Victoria and Albert Museum in London. The event was based on a traditional summer fete but with each stall given a contemporary makeover by designers and illustrators. Experience of previous years taught us the public love to get creative so participants were given three vegetables and a few additional extras to create whoever or whatever they wanted. The result was much more colourful and humorous than we could ever have imagined. Some highlights included a sweetcorn Jimmy Savile, a cabbage Dracula, a cucumber Peter Crouch and Slade's Dave Hill created from a butternut squash and some green beans.

the toploader you can open with one hand

We've made our toploader effortless to use. Its specially developed drum lid opens softly unlike ordinary spring-loaded toploaders. This way you can load it even if you only have one hand free. Try it, you'll be hooked.

GET A LIFE, GET A ZANUSSI

SPENCER WILSON
Zanussi
BBH London
2005–2007

Zanussi was a turning point for me. Until then my characters had been stumbling about on stumps... footless. I was happy with this, it was my style. However Mr Zanussi he say no... we want feet! It was make or break, I'd just had my first daughter and we needed to move so feet were added, pride was swallowed and thankfully my work changed for the positive. Just recently I've added noses, how else can you smell strawberries?

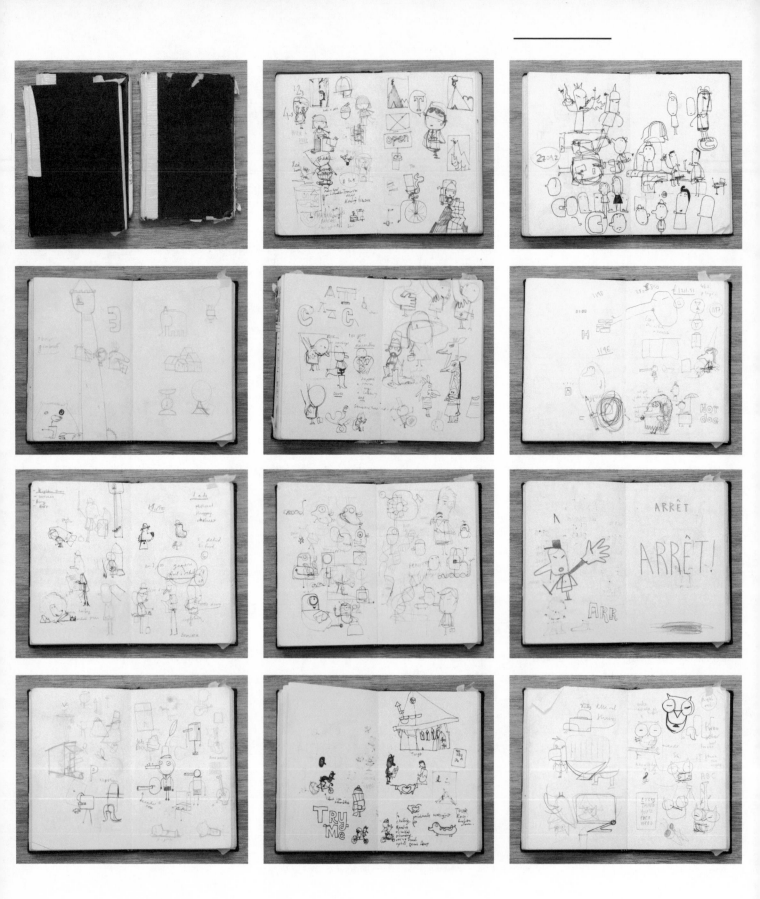

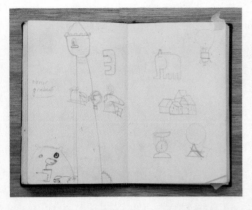

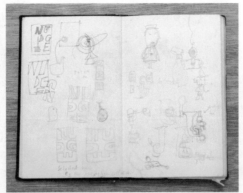

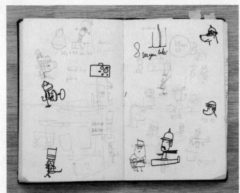

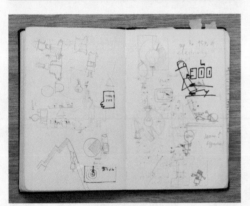

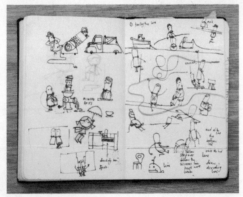

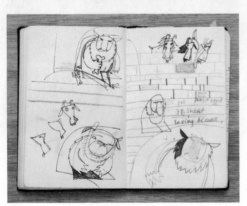

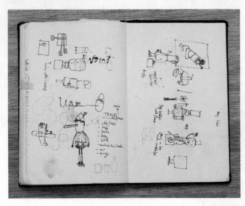

SPENCER WILSON
Sketchbooks
2009–2011

I've always struggled to keep sketchbooks. While at college, this was considered a third appendage – great big A3 ones. But since I started to work on the computer I neglected them. Instead I kept scattered thoughts on scraps of paper, bundled in boxes or filed in the bin... it was rare that I'd attach any value to them. Recently, however, I bought myself an A5 black hardback one, it's nice. I store the pencil or pen (I'm not fussy) down the spine and the paper is tough enough to escape a dunking in the bath, food and tea spillage. I've got five sketchbooks now, and when the work hits a lull I flick through and pick an idea to work up. They're still not pretty, but they're pretty useful.

SPENCER WILSON
In Print
2011

It's strange how you end up going down a certain road. My life has always had a degree of luck or someone steering me. While studying at my foundation course I stumbled into printing - having an exceptional tutor in Mike Burnett. I found that I really loved the process, the smell of the ink, the noise of the roller, the methods and the outcomes. It was Mike who suggested I should apply to Brighton and fortunately I was accepted. Whilst there, I was lucky that I found a group of friends who I still hold dear and tutors who were able to direct and push my energies. We were encouraged to try things and perhaps fail. Since then I've been lucky to receive commissions, which have afforded me a relaxed position in life and most importantly time. It's only when you have time that you can explore the things you love. I've now set up a little press, bought some inks and get work etched onto plates to relief print. When work gets repetitive or is not going well, I can glance sideways and see this set-up. Mike pops in every once and a while - he still comments on the work, offers advice and perhaps has a cup of tea in the garden.

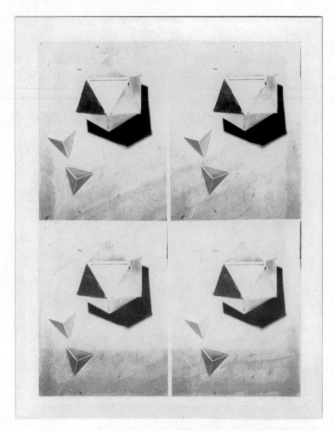

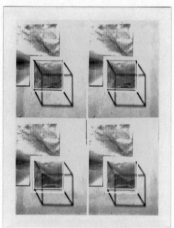
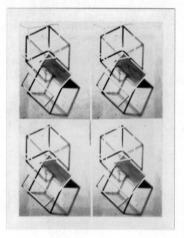
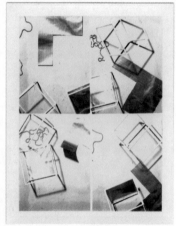

CHRISSIE MACDONALD
Experiments in Flight
2009
Photography: John Short

I produced these pieces inspired
by an article from a 1998 issue of
Raw Vision. The interview with Dr.
Evermore described his Forevertron;
an experimental machine in which he
thought he could propel himself to
the heavens on a magnetic lightening
force beam.

This series of studies – which
include maquettes and raw materials
– act as a starting point in the
development of a prototype celestial
travel vehicle. The images were
exhibited alongside the objects in
Peepshow's Inbetween show, presented
as a scientist's research cabinet of
specimens and experiments. The
photographs were to act as lo-fi
documentary studies taken by the
scientist so John suggested using
his passport Polaroid camera to
create this ephemeral look.

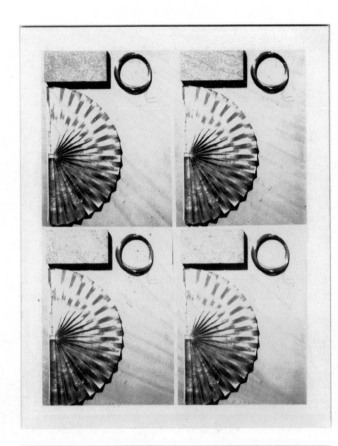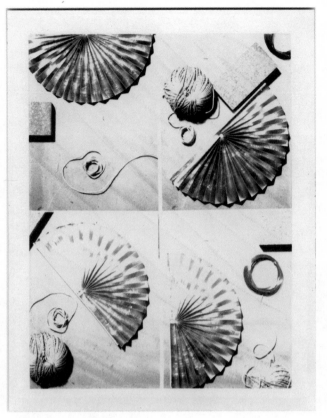

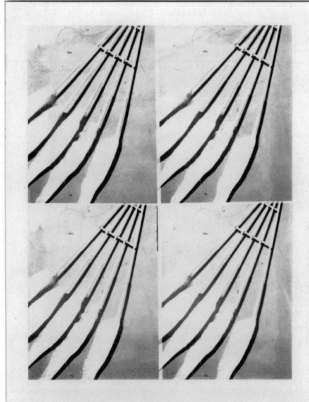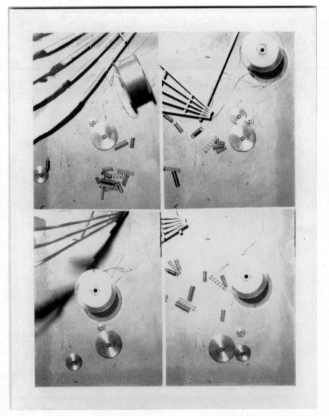

CHRISSIE MACDONALD
Overgrown
2006
Photography: John Short
John had been shooting some interiors
in a neglected building and thought
it would be a good space to use for a
still-life project. On exploring the rooms,
we noticed many of them had cracks
and upturned tiles in the floor so we
sourced these somewhat alien-looking
plant forms to grow from beneath them.

INTERVIEW Pt. 01
With Peter Nencini
Assisted by Freya Faulkner

PN: About the making or the made. The workings or the work. How you formed. I was thinking about the year 2000, when you formed. Books and studio monographs that were around at that time – the way people were thinking about illustration and graphic design. Process: A Tomato Project was published in 1996 and Rick Poynor's Design Without Boundaries in 2002. Both of them were talking about the significance of process – and that process had supplanted the solution in visual communication.

I want to ask you about what you recall of 2000 and when you started to consciously be a collective and form a studio. What do you remember about the language of illustration from that time? Not the status but the language. What you could see happening and what you were doing yourselves?

LV: It wasn't really illustration that we found exciting at the time. It was more graphic-based.

MD: Well, at college we didn't have access to the Internet. For three years, the only place we went was Brighton library. You couldn't see the work of illustrators, so much, when we were studying.

SW: (To Miles) There was the stuff that your dad would supply you with as well.

MD: Yeah, I suppose so, the 50's sci-fi and pulp magazines, Blue Note record sleeves.

LB: That's a good point. That's why we were more internal-facing. Everyone would have their sources outside that were lacking in the world of illustration and actually our own sources were more interesting.

MD: There were great books in the library but they were all painters: Basquiat, Twombly, Dubuffet.

LV: Or photographers. I mean, even the slide library we found interesting.

MD: Yeah, the slide library at Brighton was amazing. We'd spend hours in there trawling: and in the video library looking at Hitchcock movies, Saul Bass title sequences.

PN: From a chat before this question, you said that you just couldn't really see illustration. You could see it in illustration award annuals, but I guess it's inert at that point – it's got a prize but it's done and dusted. Maybe process at that time – an ongoing process out of which falls applied work – maybe that felt more exciting or more do-able?

SW: It might have been in the papers and in editorial – but because of the subject matter and how it was treated, it wasn't something that I would naturally pick up. Whereas, magazines like *The Face* were a totally different kind of thing.

LB: The Tomato book, even Mo'Wax records: they had an air of not being finished. Feasibly that something could be in-between

start and end; and that could be applied. It was quite liberating.

LV: Everything was tactile – a beautiful 'thing'.

MD: Mike Mills as well. And the Beastie Boys had a magazine called *Grand Royal* that was really exciting in the mid-nineties.

MO: I wasn't an illustration student but I would look a lot at fashion magazines. They were using photography with illustration, maybe not calling it 'illustration', but calling it 'styling' or something like that. I think, too, there was a kind of consciousness in visual communication in the late-nineties when I graduated from textiles – that things were being deconstructed. In fashion, there was a whole movement to deconstruction.

PN: The Antwerp Six.

MO: Exactly, and a lot of photographers who pared everything down. You saw the mechanics of taking a photograph or of making a garment. All that exposure of the process, I think, was prevalent – not just in illustration, but in fashion editorial and in design.

CM: I think that fed into when I started doing 3D work at Brighton. I was working on a petrol station kit – a mundane, everyday setting – and planned to build and photograph it as a design for the box. I actually then discarded the rest of it and just went with the photograph, because I realised that it was interesting in its own right. A by-product of something else.

PN: It's a good point about process. That 'by-products'– rather than the outcome you are aiming for – become the outcome.

MD: That's what happened with Marie. I mean, you got signed as an illustrator by an agency, making sketches for fashion design.

MO: Well, I was making things that were never the finished 'thing'. They were by-products of something else. In the world of communication design, people saw value in those. For me they weren't the end product; but they were, for people who were commissioning me.

LV: That 'sketchbook page' aesthetic also came out of Neasden Control Centre's work. Elevated to the final product.

PN: I know, as a group, you have enjoyed referencing vernacular drawing, vernacular forms. Non-universal sources. Some of the books around you have that about them. Pre-Google Image search, there was an enjoyment of esoteric reference.

LV: Yeah, just the ephemera that you collect along the way. I think you certainly had your box of reference, rather than the computer.

CM: It's often more about objects around you – or books that you come across – that have nothing to do with what you are really doing. Rather than going for a direct picture search on the internet, it's finding things down other routes.

AR: I was really into accidental, automatic drawing.

PN: I suppose that's what I'm thinking about. References that you wouldn't get in art school. That you wouldn't get in a linear way, you know? A type of drawing that is untrained but that is also from a communicative – or decorative – point of view, really progressive.

AR: I remember collecting together a load of drawings – on Thistle Hotel headed paper because I was working there – that actually became a formative thing for me. Stuff that I'd just been churning out without thinking about it at all.

SW: Sleep deprived, because you had to get up so early in the morning (laughter).

MO: In terms of reference, I think that everyone here has their own process, so it's not just what comes out at the end of it. With blogs, you see them as a stream of consciousness. In one way that's what's really beautiful about them. But when I studied, there was a concern over where I chose things from and how I put them together. I would take information from different disciplines or techniques and invent my own thing. A bank of reference, which is very particular to your interests.

SW: Do you share that reference? Or is it just yours?

MO: I don't know. You could discover things in a library and you kind of felt that it was yours for a little bit. Being quite insular. You grow your ideas within your own kind of perimeters.

PM: That's what keeps it interesting and keeps it moving. People have found their voice that way. We can be going another ten years and still be changing how we're influenced, finding different references and being continually interested in other things.

CM: Well for me, it took a long time to find that voice and that was the problem. I was doing things for a certain amount of time at university, then left and didn't know how it could be applied, because maybe everyone else was naturally more illustrative and I was producing this 3D work. Problems arose with the question of how to document it. I was shooting it myself, then realising that I'm not a good enough photographer. For a long while, I was trying all sorts of things to figure out where it would sit. I worked in film and window display – I did all these different jobs, to figure out its place – and came full circle. By remaining involved with Peepshow as a group – and not as my own practice – it made me realise that I could place my work in an illustration context.

MD: I still hark back to the 'Hi-Life' installation at EXPO 2000 when I realised that you didn't just have to sit and draw pictures. We had the opportunity of working with Graham Rawle; holed up in a studio in East London for the best part of a year building a 4000sq ft supermarket. We created an entire world and spent our weekends at boot sales picking up found objects to use. It became our life for a year.

PN: Was there anything else around you, alongside you in film, television, music, fashion, art, design, literature, which helped you triangulate or catalyse what you were doing, individually or collectively? BBC Three launched in 2003. Perhaps a certain sort of comedy on television? Is there anything else, where you looked at what they were doing?

AR: There was definitely in the music world. I was doing flyers. Just a way of working with friends; people who were making music or putting on nights which allowed me to have much darker themes than you'd ordinarily use in an editorial context. That's what led onto *Monkey Dust*.

ET: I suppose individually the whole Shoreditch thing, working with Neil Boorman on Shoreditch Twat and for the 333, was a massive boost to my career.

LV: It was making our own market. At the beginning, we would do all sorts of things – like the London Artists' Book Fair – and realised that we didn't really fit into that.

MD: No; that was all thousand-pound books that you had to handle with gloves.

LV: Yes, and we *wanted* to make books. That was the whole point of Peepshow at the start. We would set deadlines to make non-commercial work; and because there's a group, you've got a gun to your head. You don't want to let anyone else down.

A lot of the things that we did – sales, or little books and things like that – came out of creating our own market. There was a lot of other 'do it yourself' stuff around at the time; that was what felt quite exciting.

AR: I guess the DIY resurgence was brought on by the technology and affordability of the iMac.

PM: TV shows like Vic & Bob, Chris Morris and the League of Gentlemen... the spirit of each of these were at that time more alternative and represented an unconventional way of doing things.

MD: Michel Gondry and Spike Jonze fed into this.

AR: The Simpsons, King of the Hill and the Coen brothers' movies.

CM: Films with interesting art direction were a huge influence. That's where my interest in set design came from but also mood and lighting. The general look and feel of Jim Jarmusch's *Mystery Train* was really quite stylised; I thought it was almost like a series of still photographs made into a film.

LB: I remember *Buffalo 66* was a really important movie, because, again, it had a similar 'do-able' aesthetic.

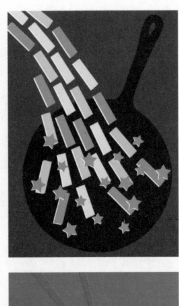
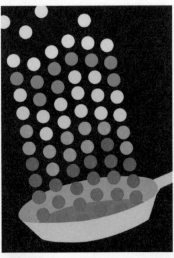

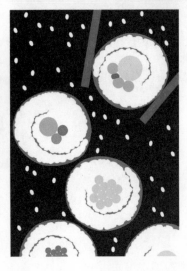

LUCY VIGRASS
Telegraph Magazine
2006–2009
I have created artwork to accompany several columns in the Telegraph Magazine over the past few years. All have inhabited the same dimensions but covered recipes, cooking techniques and environmental issues. As the illustrations were small I had to keep each image bold, boiling the copy down and keeping it simple.

LUCY VIGRASS
The Red Shoes
2010

The Lives of Others
2010

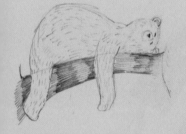

This spread
Sketches and stylings for From www to zzz

Overleaf:
Stylings for From www to zzz

PETE MELLOR (Director)
From www to zzz (1'10")
The Sleeproom
2008
With an almost completely open brief for a bed-making company, Luke settled on the idea of a bear trying to hibernate but ultimately going online and ordering a new bed from a team of birds (with an owl as their foreman). From this concept there was lots of scope for little extra shots or ideas to be included in the story, such as what are the different places that a bear would hibernate and what would prevent him sleeping? How many different ways can a team of small birds do carpentry?

0.00.00.00

0.00.03.04

0.00.06.08

0.00.09.16

0.00.10.11

0.00.12.01

0.00.14.04

0.00.16.09

0.00.17.20

0.00.19.10

0.00.21.01

0.00.22.24

0.00.24.09

0.00.26.05

0.00.28.00

0.00.29.02

0.00.30.08

0.00.31.11

0.00.32.00

0.00.33.00

0.00.34.08

0.00.35.00

0.00.35.24

0.00.36.09

0.00.38.06

0.00.38.19

0.00.40.18

0.00.42.11

0.00.43.05

0.00.44.02

0.00.45.22

0.00.46.16

0.00.47.10

0.00.50.10

0.00.51.20

0.00.53.16

0.00.55.23

0.00.58.01

0.01.02.06

0.01.02.20

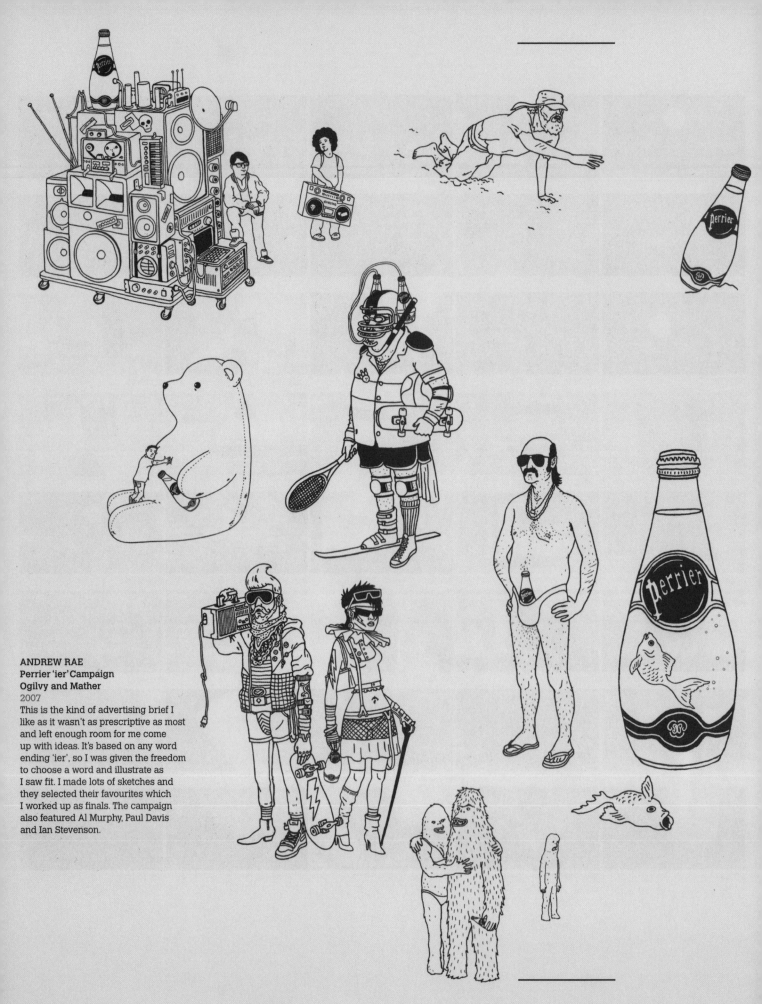

ANDREW RAE
Perrier 'ier' Campaign
Ogilvy and Mather
2007
This is the kind of advertising brief I like as it wasn't as prescriptive as most and left enough room for me come up with ideas. It's based on any word ending 'ier', so I was given the freedom to choose a word and illustrate as I saw fit. I made lots of sketches and they selected their favourites which I worked up as finals. The campaign also featured Al Murphy, Paul Davis and Ian Stevenson.

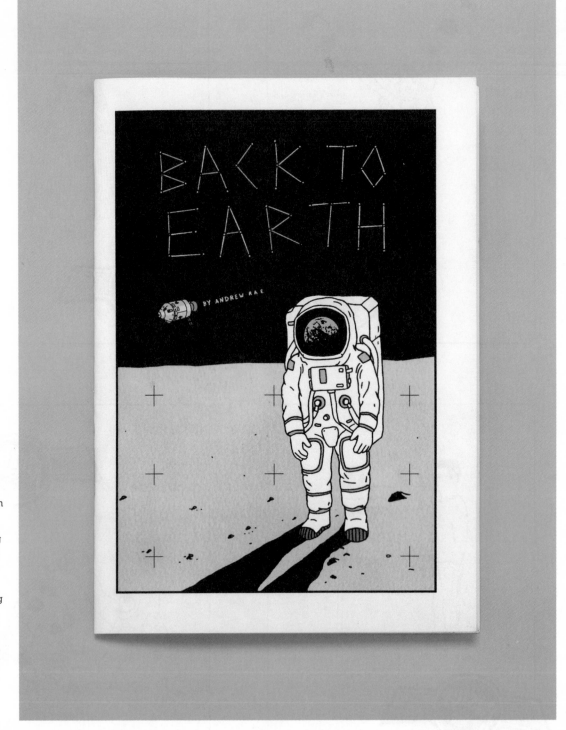

ANDREW RAE
Back To Earth Zine
2010
Years ago I saw an impressive exhibition of Moon Landing photographs at the Hayward Gallery. In the accompanying book I read about astronauts obscuring the world and everything that mattered to them with their thumbs but being unable to communicate how that made them feel. Coming home, they often felt strangely removed from what was going on around them. Ever since I had this image in my head of a lonely astronaut doing normal things at home or in the street but being separated from the world by his suit. There's something about removing the features and face that makes a character seem strangely more expressive.

Overleaf:
Last Night
2009
A page from an unfinished comic book project.

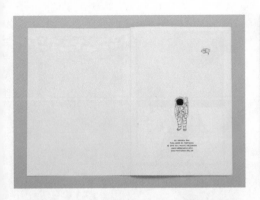
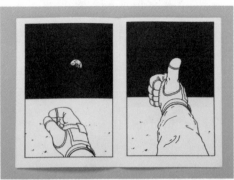

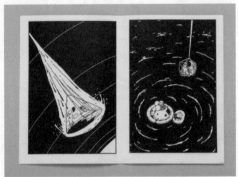

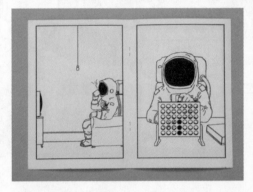
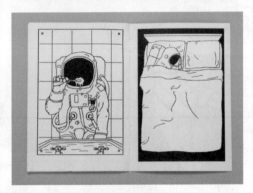

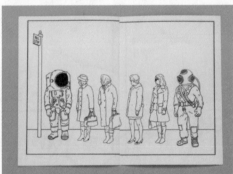

CHRISSIE MACDONALD
Ladies & Gentlemen
2010
Photography: John Short
Following on from my collaboration
with Marie on If You Could, I started
to work with wooden forms to create
figures and objects, which has been
an interesting departure from my
paper-made pieces. My personal
practice often informs my commercial
work but in this instance, the reverse
has occurred. Creating a family of
characters for the Orange campaign
has fuelled my interest in the figurative.
I enjoy using elements to suggest a
face/body/accessory, without having
to describe too much.

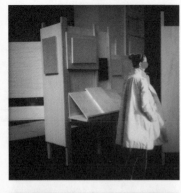

Pick Me Up
Somerset House, London
2010

We were invited to take part in Pick Me Up; the first contemporary graphic art fair in the UK. Curated by Somerset House, the event brought together the likes of Rob Ryan, Print Club London, Concrete Hermit and Nobrow for a series of workshops and activities. 14,000 visitors came through the door in 11 days.

Faced with the challenge of having no wall space on which to exhibit the work, we set about devising a series of display systems made from bare plywood and timber to house our prints, original artwork and objects. Alongside the exhibit we ran a print workshop where members of the public could create a one-of-a-kind three-colour woodblock print using pre-made blocks designed by the Peepshow team. Bespoke reversible aprons were designed and screen-printed by Jenny with a selection of patterns, to be worn on the blank side whilst printing and displayed as flags when not in use.

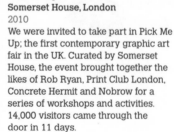

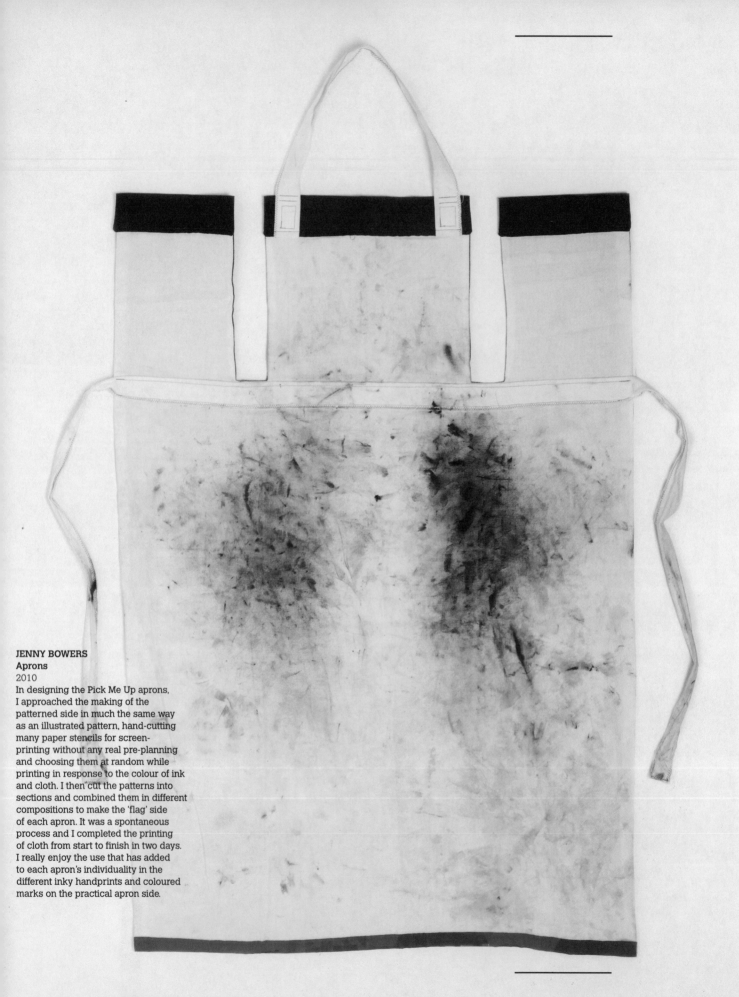

JENNY BOWERS
Aprons
2010
In designing the Pick Me Up aprons,
I approached the making of the
patterned side in much the same way
as an illustrated pattern, hand-cutting
many paper stencils for screen-
printing without any real pre-planning
and choosing them at random while
printing in response to the colour of ink
and cloth. I then cut the patterns into
sections and combined them in different
compositions to make the 'flag' side
of each apron. It was a spontaneous
process and I completed the printing
of cloth from start to finish in two days.
I really enjoy the use that has added
to each apron's individuality in the
different inky handprints and coloured
marks on the practical apron side.

Clockwise from top left:
MILES DONOVAN
Deface The Face/Madonna
HHCL/The Face
2001

I was asked to judge a competition run by The Face magazine in 2001 where readers could re-interpret a Face magazine cover; I created the portrait of Madonna as an example of what the public could do. It was one of the first pieces of work I created on my Mac. I spent ages learning how to re-interpret all the handmade processes and techniques digitally. It lead to another Deface cover for Kylie Minogue in 2003 for her book La La La, published by Hodder Stoughton.

BBC 1Xtra
Blue Source/BBC
2005

Debbie Harry
Quintet Publishing
2005

The portraits of Kraftwerk and Debbie Harry were commissioned by Quintet Publishing for the book jackets of 1001 Albums You Must Hear Before You Die. I'm excited by the prospect of being handed existing iconic imagery and re-interpreting it, putting a twist on it.

Kraftwerk
Quintet Publishing
2007

Next page:
Martin Luther King
Art Department
2009

Overleaf:
Biggie Smalls
The Source
2002

The portrait of The Notorious BIG for The Source was my very first commission via my New York agent, Art Department, in 2002. This was a big deal for me at the time; the line 'Smiles every time my face is up in The Source' appears in his track Juicy. You guessed it; I'm a big Biggie fan; as a first American commission it doesn't get much better than this.

BIGGIE SMALLS IS THE ILLEST

Ms. Wallace must be smiling. Her son's face is up in this magazine, again. But this time, it's to officially crown him as the king. The Notorious B.I.G. beat out his peers as the greatest MC of all time. And even five years after his death, he still reigns supreme.

WORDS BY KIM OSORIO
ILLUSTRATION BY MILES DONOVAN

THE BEAUTIFUL SOUTH
THE BBC SESSIONS

LUKE BEST
Beautiful South. BBC Sessions
2007
Design: Smiler Associates

Beautiful South. Live At The BBC
(Detail)
2011
Design: Smiler Associates

Overleaf:
Beautiful South. Live At The BBC
2011
Design: Smiler Associates

The starting point for both these jobs was being asked to use a previous commissioned illustration. The language of the already existing image then had to be extended to fill the formats, a fold-out for the BBC Sessions and book for Live At The BBC. The second one becomes an extension of the world created on the first cover. I started to make a night time version of the world and populated it further. Creating a set of narrative rules that govern the imagined country. Thinking what they worshipped, feared, and the conflicts that might occur in this land.

famous by the kids' art show Vision On. This has also turned up as the B-side to One Last Love Song and was unveiled live in carnival (and Guinness) mood at the Fleadh Festival in Finsbury Park.

Disc Four is a selection of some of the band's many live appearances on BBC TV. Television always welcomed The Beautiful South - perhaps it was the mix of characters that gave them a cartoonish appeal (more Simpsons than Scooby Doo it must be said), a fact the band picked up on belatedly. The group made countless appearances and PAs on long forgotten kids shows but it's fair to say they enjoyed the compliment of any invitation to do 'serious' performance on programmes like The Late Show and more memorably Later With Jools Holland.

It's hard to find any band that doesn't like the format of Later, but the Beautiful South seemed to revel in it and the compliment was regularly repaid. They were invited on to the show on five separate occasions in the decade between 1994-2004 and were also granted the honour of a Much Later of their own in 1997 that was released as a standalone DVD.

Their first appearance in December 1994 finds the band enjoying life as a runaway chart success with Carry On.... Paul Heaton has brought a new Nehru suit and Jools has long hair but the appearance stands out not for the rendition of two of their oldest songs; You Keep It All In and Let Love Speak Up Itself, but a cover of Bill Withers' You Just Can't Smile It Away. The number had been plucked from the soul man's 1985 album Watching You, Watching Me and had originally been recorded as a B-side to You Keep It All In back in 1989. Withers arguably wrote a brace of the greatest songs ever in Ain't No Sunshine and Lean On Me and was a key influence for Paul

Heaton's song writing. Funnily enough a sample from the West Virginian soul man's song Grandma's Hands appeared on the Blackstreet hit No Diggity, another song that both Heaton and Rotheray greatly admired.

The performance itself nails everything that's good about Later, in terms of a one-off moment: Jools caresses the piano, Dave Hemingway adds tempered vocal backing and Paul sings majestically. The spine-tingling moment is crowned by a sparkling saxophone solo from Courtney Pine. In one defining moment you can see the band accorded precisely the sort of respect they were frequently denied in the music press.

Of the other Later, appearances here 1996 is notable for the party atmosphere generated for popular set closer Your Father And I with the brass section dressed as wizards, and a few audience plants joining in with maracas. The November 2000 transmission has Heaton resplendent in suffocating white parka with fur collar that does nothing to diminish a terrific vocal on the hugely underrated You Can Call Me Leisure. On this occasion the band were there to publicise the release of Painting It Red, the band's 7th album that went Gold and again went to number 2. This was a sprawling album of 20 songs spread over 2cds but despite some great material (The River, Baby Please Go, 10,000 Feet) only 2 songs were released as singles. A second collection of hits followed in 2001 cheekily titled Solid Bronze, again hitting the top 10. The last Later performance, in 2004, has the band covering You're The One That I Want, this time with final co vocalist Alison Wheeler, who'd joined after the departure of Jacqui Abbot in 2003. By this point the band had been a firm fixture in the UK charts, and consequently the BBC's broadcasting schedule for 15 years.

DVD

Top of the Pops 10/01/93
1 OLD RED EYES IS BACK
Written by Paul Heaton and Dave Rotheray.
Published by Island Music Ltd. ℗ 2011 BBC.

The Late Show 2/8/90
2 BELL BOTTOMED TEAR
Written by Paul Heaton and Dave Rotheray.
Published by Island Music Ltd. ℗ 2011 BBC.

The Late Show 2/8/90
3 WE'LL DEAL WITH YOU LATER
Written by Paul Heaton and Dave Rotheray.
Published by Island Music Ltd. ℗ 2011 BBC.

Later with Jools Holland 9/12/94
4 YOU KEEP IT ALL IN
Written by Paul Heaton and Dave Rotheray.
Published by Island Music Ltd. ℗ 2011 BBC.

Later with Jools Holland 9/12/94
5 YOU JUST CAN'T SMILE IT AWAY
Written by Bill Withers.
Published by Blenny Music Inc. ℗ 2011 BBC.

Later with Jools Holland 9/12/94
6 LET LOVE SPEAK UP ITSELF
Written by Paul Heaton and Dave Rotheray.
Published by Island Music Ltd. ℗ 2011 BBC.

Later with Jools Holland 16/11/96
7 DON'T MARRY HER
Written by Paul Heaton and Dave Rotheray.
Published by Island Music Ltd. ℗ 2011 BBC.

Later with Jools Holland 16/11/96
8 BLACKBIRD ON THE WIRE
Written by Paul Heaton and Dave Rotheray.
Published by Island Music Ltd. ℗ 2011 BBC.

Later with Jools Holland 26/11/98
9 PERFECT 10
Written by Fred Neil. Published by
Published by Universal-Island Music Ltd. ℗ 2011 BBC.

Later with Jools Holland 26/11/98
10 WINDOW SHOPPING FOR BLINDS
Written by Paul Heaton and Dave Rotheray.
Published by Island Music Ltd. ℗ 2011 BBC.

Later with Jools Holland 26/11/98
11 YOUR FATHER AND I
Written by Paul Heaton and Dave Rotheray.
Published by Island Music Ltd. ℗ 2011 BBC.

Later with Jools Holland 2000
12 ROTTERDAM
Written by Paul Heaton and Dave Rotheray.
Published by Island Music Ltd. ℗ 2011 BBC.

November 2000 2000
13 OLD RED EYES IS BACK
Written by Paul Heaton and Dave Rotheray.
Published by Island Music Ltd. ℗ 2011 BBC.

Later with Jools Holland 18/11/00
14 CLOSER THAN MOST
Written by Paul Heaton and Dave Rotheray.
Published by Island Music Ltd. ℗ 2011 BBC.

Later with Jools Holland 18/11/00
15 THE RIVER
Written by Paul Heaton and Dave Rotheray.
Published by Island Music Ltd. ℗ 2011 BBC.

Later with Jools Holland 18/11/00
16 YOU CAN CALL ME LEISURE
Written by Paul Heaton and Dave Rotheray.
Published by Island Music Ltd. ℗ 2011 BBC.

Later with Jools Holland 22/5/04
17 YOU'RE THE ONE THAT I WANT
Written by John Farrar. Published by
Sony / ATV Music Publishing (UK). ℗ 2011 BBC.

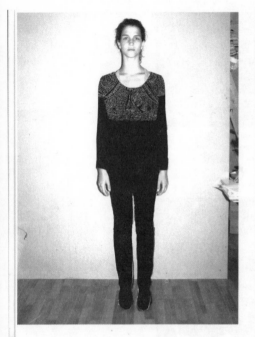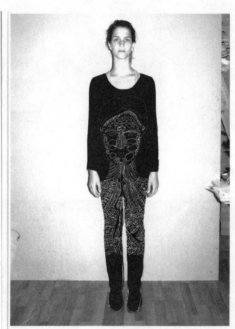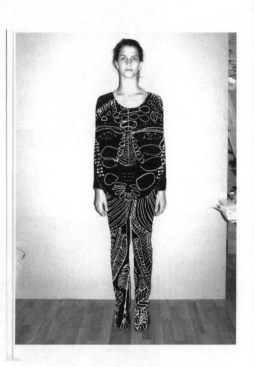

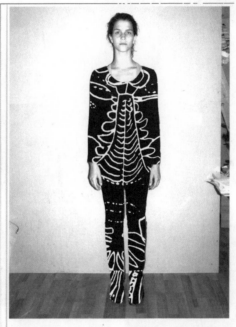

MARIE O'CONNOR
Drawn Thread Work
Detroit Gallery, Stockholm
2010

I was invited by Fashionplay to participate in their annual fashion event in Stockholm. A drawing for a tattoo made by a native of Easter Island, found in the 1947 book Are Clothes Modern? An essay on contemporary apparel, became the starting point for this project. The line-up came about by employing a typical technique for me – using a cut-out body template, which is laid over images or objects. In this instance there was thought with the initial placement; the first outfit being determined by placing the tattooed face where a real face would be. The remaining pattern falls onto the body creating a print on the shoulders and torso. The subsequent outfits are enlargements of the face and its position moves around the wearer's body.

As the image grows, so too does the textile treatment. Screen print, fabric appliqué, carved wood, clay embellishment and more were used in an attempt to explore different qualities of line and ways to draw in material. As well as the various treatments, the garments' construction also grew in complexity, with the drawing itself dictating the design and shapes within each outfit. The neck falling below the hips became pockets, the enlarged nose area of the face suggested a jacket.

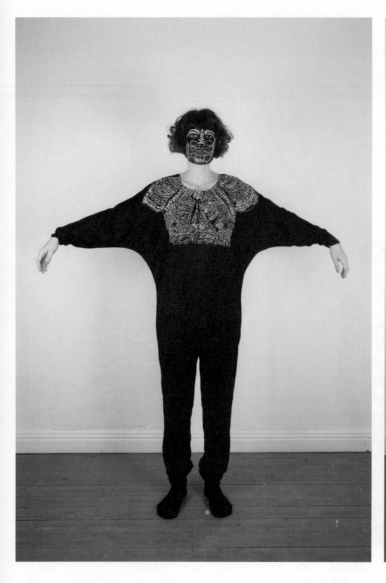

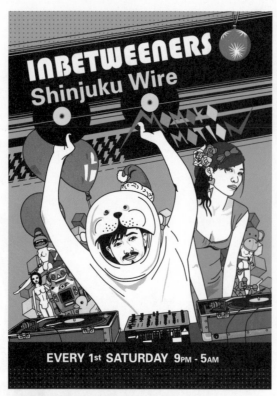

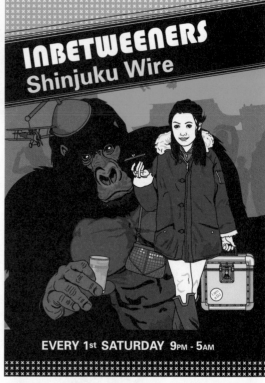

ELLIOT THOBURN
Inbetweeners
Naoki Kato
2010-2011

I love the ephemeral quality of flyers; they are like small snapshots of moments in culture. They can tell you a great deal about a certain time or scene. With flyers I have always tried to make references to current trends, events or fashions at that time. This could be a nod to a film, world politics or something as trivial as a lot of girls in Shoreditch trying to look like Stevie Nicks.

For example, the naked man on the Inbetweeners flyer is a famous singer-presenter-actor in Japan who the month before had got drunk and naked in the local kids park in the early hours of the morning. He was on the news apologising for quite some time after. There's a story about the girl next to him too.

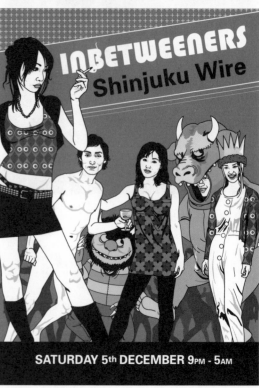

ELLIOT THOBURN
Notion Hipster Handbook
Notion Magazine
2007

CHRISSIE MACDONALD
Edinburgh Fringe Festival
Programme + Poster imagery
2008
Design & Art Direction: Marque
Photography: John Short

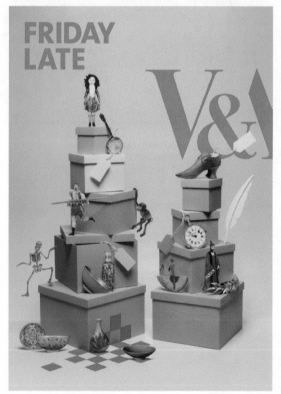

CHRISSIE MACDONALD
V&A Friday Late
2010–2011
Photography: John Short
Additional content photography
supplied by the V&A
These seasonal poster and postcard
images illustrate a programme of
themed events held in the Victoria and
Albert Museum. Each piece represents
three to four different evenings and had
to be cropped to focus on the individual
events while still functioning as an
entire image.

I am my older sister and unfortunately my younger brother.

search online for 'I am'

orange

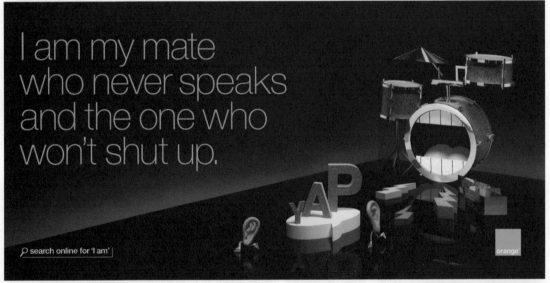

I am my mate who never speaks and the one who won't shut up.

search online for 'I am'

orange

I am who I am because of everyone.

search online for 'I am'

orange

CHRISSIE MACDONALD
Orange 'I Am' campaign
Agency: Fallon London
2008–2011
Photography: John Short
This campaign has been pretty extraordinary in many ways. When it first began in May 2008 I could never have anticipated the momentum it would gain over the coming years. It all started on one very long night of crafting and shooting some test images with John to present to Fallon the following morning. After many hours in the studio I had my 'Eureka' moment… let's put feet on it! I exclaimed. And the rest is history.

The period between this shoot and final go-ahead was a busy one. It was apparent I'd need to enlist the help of skilled makers to work alongside me throughout the campaign and thankfully Alex Bec was working with Peepshow at the time. The font-of-all-knowledge when it comes to creative talent, he introduced me to some amazing designers and together with a few I also had in mind, my band of merry makers was formed. Now I just needed a mastermind to manage and produce the whole operation. That's where another Alex – Plaza – came in.

With the team in place it was also clear that I would need a lot more room than the Peepshow studio would allow so I established myself in a new location a stone's throw from John's studio. And so it began…

More extraordinary than the longevity of the campaign is both the creative as well as personal relationships forged between everyone involved. The agency and client had a great deal of foresight and the input from John and I was acknowledged and respected.

Following three spreads:
PETE MELLOR (Director)
Growing Together – CBeebies (4 x 40")
RedBee Media/BBC
2007–2009

The scripts we received from Red
Bee Media for the Growing Together
promotainments were open enough for
us to put our own thoughts and ideas
into the process. After winning the pitch
with lots of sketches, stylings and an
animation test, we set about the task
of refining the look of the animations
and also creating a cast of characters
to inhabit the worlds we were creating.
Internally everyone pitched characters
- often stepping outside of how they
would normally work - and settled on
a small team to create the majority
of the artwork and to art-direct the
various extra elements provided by
others. We had heavily story-boarded
and styled the scenes prior to the live
action shoot but of course some things
had to be flexible as we were dealing
with one unknown and unpredictable
element - working with young children.
The final films were a mix of techniques
and textures - stop-frame animated
fish, rocks made from sponges, painted
grass, drawn trees and CGI ladybirds.

IMAGINE CHILDREN'S FESTIVAL
12 – 27 FEBRUARY 2011
SOUTHBANK CENTRE

JEREMY STRONG
Tuesday 22 February

Top children's author Jeremy Strong kicks off his Year of Fun campaign with readings from Cartoon Kid, a superhero extravaganza packed with his slapstick humour. Everyone in Mr Butternut's class has to choose their superhero name – this is your chance to learn about Casper the Cartoon Kid and Big Feet Pete. You can ask Jeremy questions and then meet him in person at the book signing afterwards.

Suitable for ages seven and over

'Comedy and fizz are
Jeremy Strong's trademarks.'
(The Independent)

Purcell Room at Queen Elizabeth Hall, 2.30pm
£6 (adults) £4 (children)

ANTHONY BROWNE
Wednesday 23 February

Children's Laureate Anthony Browne is the creator of Gorilla, Silly Billy and Willy the Wimp. Join him for this intructive show about looking, drawing and dreaming. Watch Anthony at work as he takes us on a magical journey through an imaginative landscape, drawing his characters live and asking you to help create stories with him.

Suitable for ages five and over

Purcell Room at Queen Elizabeth Hall, 2.30pm
£6 (adults) £4 (children)

DAN ZANES AND FRIENDS
Thursday 24 – Sunday 27 February

All the way from Brooklyn, New York, and back by popular demand after a sold-out run of shows in 2008, Dan Zanes and Friends bring their festive style of 21st-century, all-ages handmade family music to Southbank Centre.

Dan and his band are joined by special guests including a London youth orchestra created especially for these shows. The wild sounds of electric guitar, fiddle, drums, trumpet, upright bass, harmonica, spoons, mandolin, voices and orchestra are sure to rouse everyone into an all-ages dance party frenzy.

'Dan Zanes is the Pied Piper of the family music scene... by some distance the best of this new breed of children's entertainer.'
(The Times)

Suitable for all ages

Queen Elizabeth Hall, 11am & 2pm
£12

British Sign Language interpreted performance by Martin Roberts on Saturday 26 February, 2pm.

IMAGINE CHILDREN'S FESTIVAL

Join us for a fun-filled February at Imagine, where musicians, storytellers, comedians, puppeteers and dancers create our annual children's festival. Hear from the best children's authors and then meet them after the shows, take part in free workshops with artists from around the world and help us to create Old Possum's Book of Practical Cats – a musical and poetry show taking shape on The Clore Ballroom at Royal Festival Hall. Join us on our journey of artistic discovery at Imagine.

All listings correct at time of going to press.

THE FLYING MACHINE 3D
WORLD EXCLUSIVE PREVIEW SCREENINGS
Saturday 12 & Sunday 13 February

A spectacular new 3D film adventure for the whole family, The Flying Machine is a modern fairy tale combining live action and stop motion animation.

Starring Heather Graham and super-star pianist Lang Lang, who also performs the soundtrack, the film is inspired by Chopin's timeless, unforgettable music. One family must take to the skies to travel home, criss-crossing the world in an action-packed, life-affirming adventure from Academy Award-winning producer Hugh Welchman.

Royal Festival Hall
Saturday 12 February, 7.30pm
Red carpet tickets £25, £20
Sunday 13 February, 10am, 1pm, 3pm & 6pm
£15 £12.50
Concessions 50% off (limited availability)

Brought to you by Sky 3D and presented by BreakThru Films

SPENCER WILSON
Imagine Children's Festival
Southbank Centre
2011
With two young daughters, my work has slowly been infiltrated with the visuals from childrens' books. I'm drawn to them in much the same way as when I was a kid. Studying the little nuances, the colours, the characterisation, the compositions and finding the extras the illustrator had hidden... the slow burner – all while sitting snug in a bed with two fidgety children. When this project came along, it allowed me to dip into this vault. The brief was open but still informed by the copy and I tried to have some fun with it. I showed the finished thing to the girls, it's always nice to see their reaction to what daddy does.

SPENCER WILSON
Music Man
2011

Accordian
Polga
2010

LUCY VIGRASS
Lego
2010

Opposite:
Lego Fabric Hanging
2010
This was created for Pick Me Up
2010. Designed using a job lot of
Lego bought on E-bay and transcribed
into a fabric patchwork.

Overleaf:
Meccano
2008
I have always enjoyed accidental
design. This image is one of a series
based on photographs of 'job-lots' for
sale on eBay. There is a beauty in the
way a seller lays out a group of objects
for display, be it meccano, stamps or
electrical components.

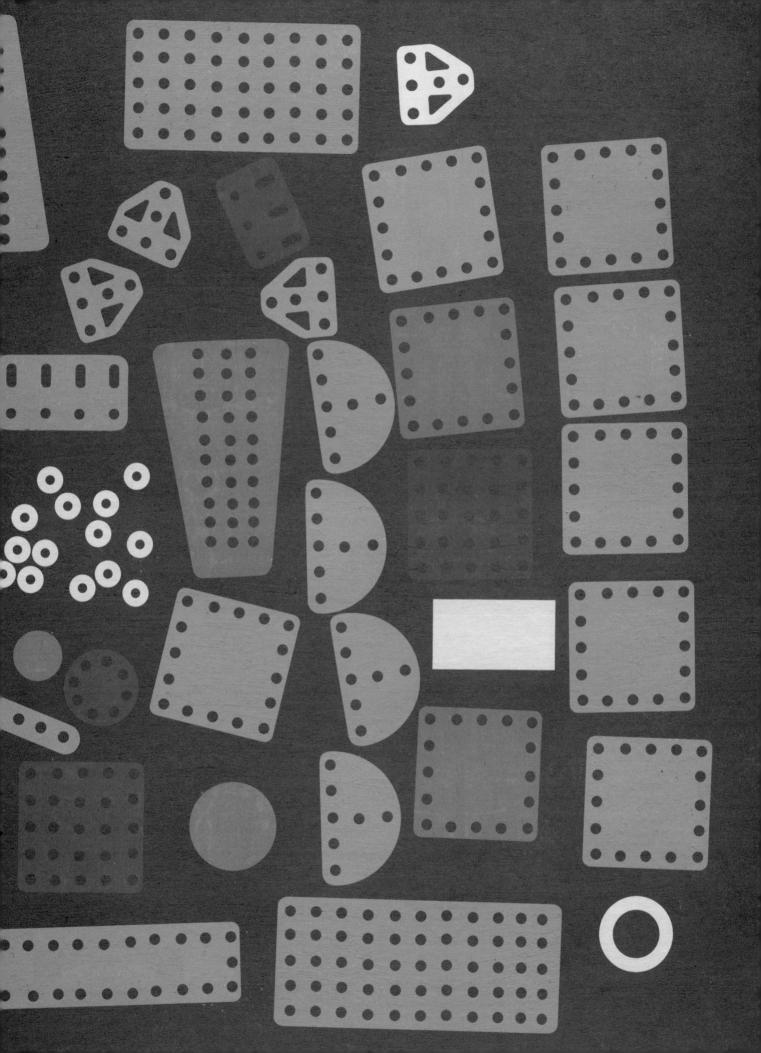

CHRISSIE MACDONALD
& MARIE O'CONNOR
If You Could: Collaborate
A Foundation Gallery /
Rochelle School, London
It's Nice That
2010

Chrissie was invited to participate in the fourth annual incarnation of If You Could; this time an exhibition exploring the act of collaboration, bringing together 33 partnerships across many diverse specialisms. Inviting Marie to be her creative sidekick, the pair initially set out with their common interests and a whole heap of collected materials such as wooden rods, pulp balls, lollipop sticks, plasticine and more and began making small studies. Some became figurative, some remained ambiguous. Feeling their way through the process and seeing where the experiments would take them, they moved onto a larger scale, approaching the making in a similar way to create a series of forms out of salvaged wood and scrap material. Using off-cuts and pieces that had been pre-determined by another's hand, the pair translated these inherited shapes into 3D collage constructions.

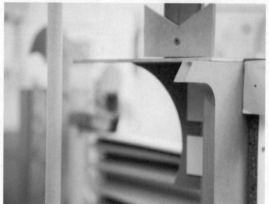

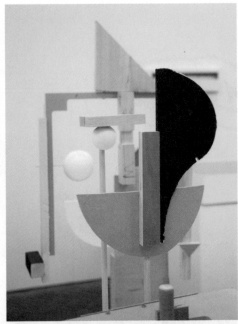
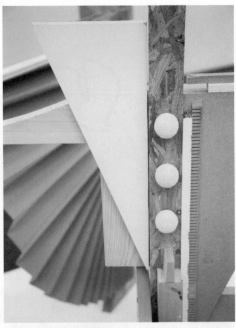

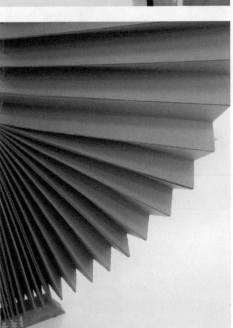

ANDREW RAE
Vice UK and Vice Espana
2011

ANDREW RAE
Print Magazine
2009

ANDREW RAE
Perverted Science
2000–2003
I made a monthly flyer for the Perverted Science club night at 333 in Shoreditch at the beginning the century. It told a loose story of The Meaver, a hybrid beast (half-moose and half-beaver) on a rampage in East London. The series culminated in a group exhibition at Dreambagsjaguarshoes.

It's just a matter of time

PUL
SE E

MILES DONOVAN
Access
Wire Design
2005

MILES DONOVAN
33 Revolutions per Minute
Faber & Faber
2010

The Billion Dollar Bubble
Financial Times
2009

MILES DONOVAN
Made In China
Creative Review
2008

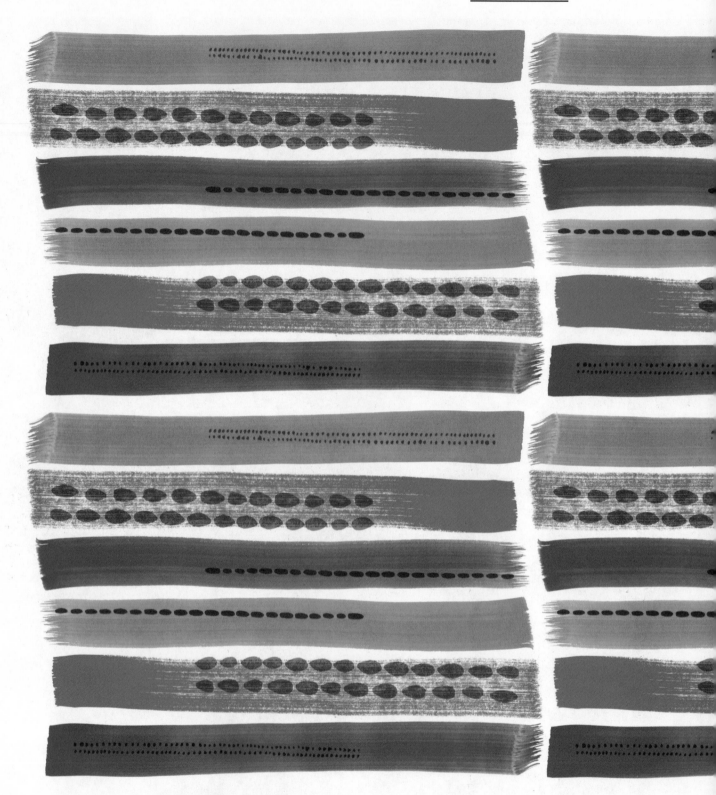

JENNY BOWERS
Afternoon Tea, Japan
2011
Afternoon Tea commissioned me
to create a set of designs to reflect
'London'. They had some specific
ideas that I expanded on, combining
London icons with sections of pattern.
The work was applied to a series of
products from tumblers to clocks
to blankets.

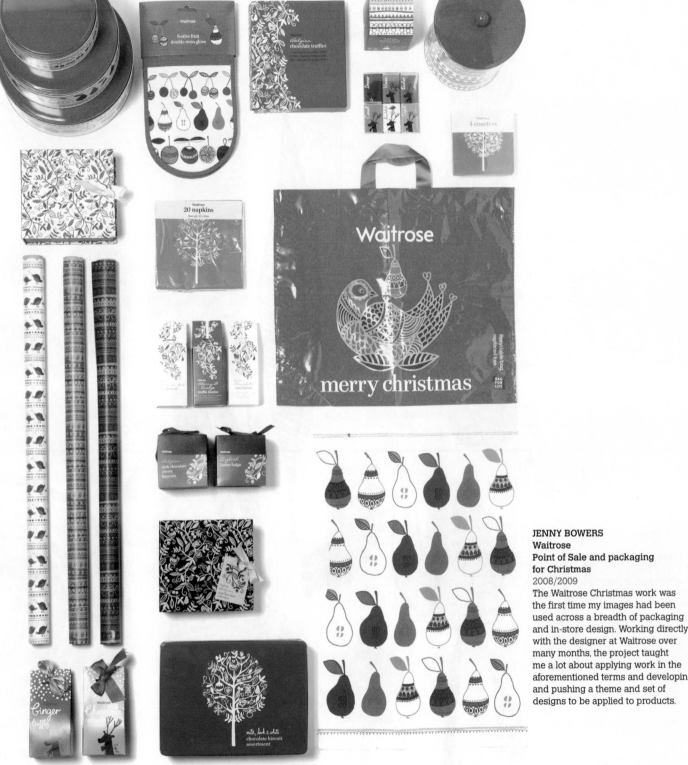

JENNY BOWERS
Waitrose
Point of Sale and packaging
for Christmas
2008/2009
The Waitrose Christmas work was
the first time my images had been
used across a breadth of packaging
and in-store design. Working directly
with the designer at Waitrose over
many months, the project taught
me a lot about applying work in the
aforementioned terms and developing
and pushing a theme and set of
designs to be applied to products.

JENNY BOWERS
Senses
Don't Panic
2004
This image was an important piece
of work when I started to receive
commissions, in that it seemed to
appeal to a number of clients
who used this image as reference.
People seemed to enjoy the
playfulness of the combination
of images and the mix of media.

Opposite page:
Ski village
Roxy
2006

INTERVIEW Pt. 02
With Peter Nencini
Assisted by Freya Faulkner

There's this big issue in illustration about the 'moment of choice': from a text; from a narrative. But there is a sense, sometimes, in your work of an incidental moment. Slightly the wrong moment. Or a moment when somebody is wandering off the edge of the page. So it's about seeing the workings of things. I wonder it that helps with what you are trying to say in the image?

MO: The 'point of choice' – I don't know whether or not you mean, or include, when you decide to stop. When I am making, I'm not thinking consciously: "Oh this looks a little bit awkward." When you decide to leave it, can be the hardest thing. When it's finished or not finished. Sometimes you have to go overboard and then take it back again. There's a kind of conversation with the image that you are making, all of the time. I don't think I am consciously making something that appears to be unfinished, or that appears to have that lightness or awkwardness. But emotionally, it feels right.

PN: Yes, nimbleness and lightness – the idea that the work is nimble in some way – that there are permutations. When this one was made, there are others; and they are equal in weight. It's not like there's the 'bull's eye' solution, or something.

FF: Is there also something about risk taking? About not necessarily continuing down a road with something and nailing it to the floor but actually taking the risk of leaving it slightly unfinished and exposing some of the mechanisms behind it and leaving that gap? You were talking about how, in the illustration annuals, with this really resolved, finished work, it just completely turned you off and you didn't touch it with a barge pole. Is there something about the excitement of a risk? Maybe you're naturally drawn to having that sort of gap.

MO: Yeah; I think personally I like ambiguity in the work and when something is *just about* to become something. Having that point of ambiguity.

AR: I started using the computer, in collaging my own work. I would do as many drawings as I could, pick out the good ones and then just start to collage them together. Putting things together and seeing how that worked. Just enjoying the composition. I guess that has the same awkwardness about it.

SW: My work is driven by the programme I use: Adobe Illustrator. I'd just have a massive artboard and stick loads of stuff around it; that's how the whole illustration evolves. I might just drag the entire body and leave an arm, or take a bit, then open up another file, copy another file onto that artboard, then start taking those bits apart to create my drawing. While I'm doing all of that, my brain might be somewhere else or listening to music. Then accidental things occur where, for example, I've accidentally clicked on the background and dragged it across. That changes the composition. I take a complete copy, move it over and then work on that. I do, though, have a certain amount of rules in my work.

LB: Most of the illustration we looked at, we felt, was really dead-ended. So I guess that – in subconscious reaction – we all made work with the influence of painting, or record covers. Things that feel as if they have a life beyond and before. The work we make – although it is to communicate a specific thing in an editorial for example – it has more open-endedness. The other reason is that we all consciously make about ten to twenty versions of the image before making that decision. So process is important.

PN: Do you submit those as well?

LB: No; but I think we all have a strong work ethic. Which is another point. So it feels like there are ten other versions. Chrissie's characters for Orange: they belong to a whole family and she probably designed a lot more than were ever seen to get to that point. You can tell, in the work, that it has a bigger world around it, because we all make that much work.

SW: What I always found annoying is that traditionally the illustrator would work out a pencil version of the piece and then just copy that in colour. That would just kill me. That would be so boring.

PN: But has anything been lost, in the commitment to a create an idea? To the killer idea? Or perhaps the conditions for that to happen don't exist anymore.

SW: Well, I think it's a marriage between me and the person commissioning. If they're good, then they'll get the best from me.

LV: There is a problem now – working commercially – that people commissioning you think that every image you make is infinitely changeable because of the computer. I think, in some ways, you lose a bit of ownership in what is that final image.

MO: I think maybe the idea of a kit of parts is relevant to all of us. That we have a kind of reservoir, a bank of stuff, whether that's physical stuff; or a knowledge of reference; or a spreadsheet of limbs; or colours and textures; or there's a framework to work within. If you have that 'catalogue' then you can allow yourself to be playful within that. You can do things quickly, because you've got the means to do it. I find that I've got a bit of confidence if I've got the specific kit I need for a specific job. Then it's about responding to the kit that you've acquired.

PN: It allows you the conditions to create flexible work.

LV: Also, it's your own parameters.

PN: And you won't be 'killed' by someone saying it doesn't work, because you have spare matter.

MO: It's a vocabulary that can expand, be reduced or constantly evolve. Doing that with hands but even on screen, there's the idea that everything is mobile and interchangeable.

LV: I have the same rules using the computer that I would have outside the computer. Otherwise it's not my language anymore.

MD: When I'm working, I will save the job after two hours, then four hours, then six hours. At the six-hour stage, I often open those documents and sit there and go: "Right; well I like this, this and this." I'll create a kind of 'monster' out of those three things and then go forward with it, sometimes through the same process again.

PN: The aspect that can often be least talked about – if we're talking about evident process – is the fact that all of this is visual communication. It's for editorial; it's statement making. Your processing behaviours: do they help in the communication of content? If you are doing an editorial, does it help in breaking a cliché?

For example, Luke: the idea that it's a moment just after, or just before; or you imagine somebody has just turned away; or the composition is off-kilter. The idea that, then, you are putting yourself to the side of the classic 'moment of choice,' or 'the well-trodden path,' in a solution for a business editorial.

LB: Yeah. I guess that's my chosen approach to doing an editorial. It's not my only approach, because I can't design the cliché well enough. Ultimately, I'm more interested in narrative; I'll always solve it with a narrative. So it will always have that moment.

CM: I enjoy creating work that gives the sense that something has happened before or after it. Like a film still. I remember Cindy Sherman has likened her images to stills from a film, where they suggest a whole other narrative going on around them, without having to make the rest of the film. I like the idea that it is a moment where something just happened or might happen.

LV: I think I'm probably more solution-based. I quite like to tie it all up in one neat package, with a bow on it, probably.

PN: Superficially, your work is reductive and graphic but it's made out of parts that waver a little bit. There is something else going on there. It's not as locked down as that. There's something that 'wobbles' a bit more. Or it feels as if the individual forms aren't the 'absolute' forms; some of them might be more ephemeral. So it's editorial and it's still saying something and it is a solution but there's some kind of doubt in there, I think.

LV: It probably goes back to the reference material, as well. I think of the solution and then I'll picture research but then it goes laterally. I get lost for a day wandering around in different worlds on the Internet.

LB: You are an amazing picture researcher. You've got a real skill at it. Going beyond the keyword and actually getting to the less obvious.

CM: Yeah, it's how you do your research that really has depth.

LV: Well you just get lost in other people's worlds, don't you?

PN: I'm thinking now about the way that people who've commissioned you have understood what you do. Is the process the idea? Is the process commissioned? When people who've seen 'Village Fête' and have seen you operate in that way – or when they come to your studio to brief – do you think they are interested in asking you, somewhat, to 'do what you do'?

LV: You can get someone who is interested in what you do but they haven't got the project that it's right for. But they want to use you anyway. That's when things can go wrong.

LB: There's definitely not enough weight on the process; on the ideas part of any project. There's more weight and time on the finishing of something.

PM: On an animation level, we put a lot of thought into the concept and narrative. In a recent job, we rewrote a bit of their script; we added more; we worked out every second of the two and a half minutes in the pub. I think that's a real strength of ours. We do have a good idea of what we want to present to someone. It's a shame sometimes when you're not given the time to fully round it off.

PN: There's a certain fluency that happens with the animation. You've talked in previous interviews of it as the exception; the moment when you as a group are at your optimum. When something else happens.

MD: It's quite often the only time that we truly collaborate on things now. We do all sit down and discuss — with whoever is available — the idea, the scripts and then do it collectively. Not all of those people will go away and carry on with the project — it might just be two or three people who work it out afterwards — but that initial discussion is really exciting.

AR: That discussion does often happen when we are producing our own work as well.

LB: The difference with animation, Village Fête, Pick Me Up and other events — maybe this has taken a while for us to get to, in terms of maturity as a group — is they work better because everyone lets go of their visual language more. Actually, then, you engage more in the process and the idea.

AR: Which is a real treat as an illustrator — to be able to step outside of your style — because you just get so pigeonholed.

MD: On the Saatchi windows project, it was explaining a working process across the building. It was an idea of Lucy's that was passed on to Luke, who found ways of building things. Then I took what Luke did and started making it myself. It was a quite organic and interesting process.

LV: I find that what we do collaboratively in Peepshow is the only time that I probably 'play', outside of what I do commercially. I'd like to think that I would make work for myself but the prints, the Lego compositions, are still for Peepshow. If you took all that away, would I still make work just for myself? Illustration? Probably not. I'm actually excited about the fact that I'm going to have to make stuff for my daughter but it's for her; it won't be for me. I wouldn't do it for myself, because, you know, I exist within a brief.

AUBIN
&
WILLS

LUKE BEST
Almanac Magazine
Aubin & Wills
2010

Clockwise from left:
LUKE BEST
Job Hopping
Harvard Business Review
2010

Hoarding
Globe and Mail Magazine
2010

Iowa
Harpers Magazine
2010

Over the years, editorial illustration has become a big part of my practice but one that still intimidates and excites me. With quick deadlines and problem-solving being key, the aesthetic becomes secondary, allowing for a different mode of work to take place. It's taken a lot of practice but I've started to make images that communicate in a manner that is true to my visual thinking. Looking back over the work there is a clear method emerging. I try to create a small visual narrative as my solution, rather than a quick direct clear message. I want the viewer to have to work a bit and where possible, spend the same time with the image as they do with the article.

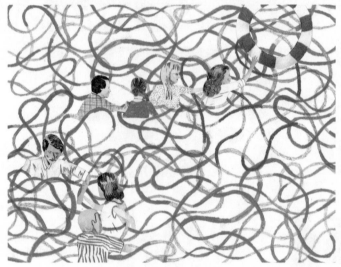

Clockwise from top left:
LUKE BEST
Prison Education
The Guardian
2009

Carl Akeley The Taxidermist
Washington Post
2010

Tracey
World of Interiors
2011

Social Workers
The Guardian
2008

ELLIOT THOBURN
Difficult Clients
Digital Arts Magazine
2009

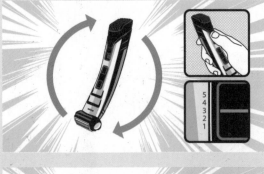

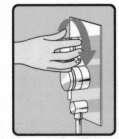

PETE MELLOR & CHRIS SAYER
(Directors)
ELLIOT THOBURN (Art Director)
MILES DONOVAN (Art Director)
How to be King... (11 x 1')
DDB Tribal/Philips
2010–2011

The beauty of this profession is that you are always learning through the pursuit of problem-solving: even if the solution involves applying make-up to a man in his pants, you can take something away from it. But 11 one-minute-long animations turned round in a limited amount of time is no easy task. Add to this an illustration style that doesn't lend itself naturally to animation, the aforementioned man in his pants and three different time zones – the agency in Amsterdam, Peepshow in London and Elliot in Japan – and you end up with a steep learning curve.

This job was a real team effort: Pete and Miles with Chris (from production company Wyld Stallyons) had to make the illustrations move in an effective way within an exceptionally tight timeframe. Some creative storyboarding and efficient live shoots made the job of illustrating easier than expected.

The different time zones ended up being an advantage – Elliot being eight hours ahead allowed him to get a lot done before the animators even got out of bed.

The last illustrations were sent to the UK during a rather large aftershock, some hours after a big earthquake had hit Japan.

ELLIOT THOBURN
333 Saturdays
Off Centre
2003–2005

DEVIL'S DANDRUFF

GUIDE TO NIGHTLIFE

By Neil Boorman & Daniel Pemberton
Illustrations by Elliot Thoburn

ELLIOT THOBURN
Devil's Dandruff Guide To Nightlife
Gerald Duckworth & Co
2005
Ultimately born out of the Shoreditch
Twat, Devil's Dandruff started as a
column in The Guardian Guide, running
for one year, before being published
as a book in 2005. The book was a real
collective effort, with Neil Boorman
(founder of the Shoreditch Twat) and
Daniel Pemberton (club journalist and
writer on the Twat) doing the vast
majority of the writing. All of us worked
together to achieve the best we could
in the limited time we had available.

The book itself, like the column
which preceded it, is an illustrated
and humorous guide to one of modern
Britain's favourite activities – going
out. Similar in some respects to a
nature guide, it tells you how to spot
the myriad of species – from
undercover policemen to bolshy
cloakroom girls – that inhabit the club
scene; how to dance; how to blag your
way in and much more. We tried to
cover every aspect of contemporary
nightlife culture, both high and low.

The club scene is always evolving and
some aspects of the book six years on
may now seem a little dated, however
most of the general themes and ideas
still ring true, especially the people.
I love drawing people and this is a book
full of people, warts and all. It's really
nice to be asked to draw the not-so-
beautiful and comment on the world
I inhabit.

The turnaround for a lot of the
illustrations was very quick and it was
probably the most intense time in my
working life. That also goes for the two
designers – Phil Seddon and Fiorella
Lee – who both put up with all the legal
changes and tight deadlines, amongst
other things.

The majority of the illustrations are
based on our experiences and real
observations – that's who they were
and what they were like, with a little
bit of artistic license.

DEVIL'S DANDRUFF

● Bedroom DJ *Juvenae Masterbatum*

A close relative of Box Boy and extremely distant cousin of Superstar DJ, the bedroom variety is a brooding adolescent who shuns traditional paths of employment, personal development and dalliances with love in favour of the almighty deck, mixer and Faithless 12". Typically found in the bedroom furthest away from his parents in the family home (Dad isn't a big fan of early DJ Hell), this solitary species repeats an endless cycle of rituals at his home-made temple in the hope that one day he might, just might, become the new Brandon Block. This species often displays abnormal behavioural traits for a male in his late adolescence. While most healthy boys would have posters of Ferraris and Abi Titmuss on their walls, Bedroom DJ opts for promotional posters of expensive scratch needles and turntable equipment. Indeed, the same can be said for mix tapes; giving existing and prospective girlfriends two-hour journeys into Tribal House as opposed to the traditional Nick Drake/ Coldplay/ Brian Eno combo. Rarely spotted inside a club (unless it's to see a touring scratch champion), but can be identified by sun-starved skin, hairy palms and threadbare Nervous Records t-shirt.

Daily Routine

1. Rewire cartridges
2. Buff brass plack on limited edition Technics
3. Re-alphabetise records
4. Buff and re-alphabetise collection of pornography
5. Reread and memorise a chapter from 24hr Party People
6. Review scratch technique on digi camera
7. Record new tunes in log book
8. Watch girls walk to/from school out of window
9. Buff and re-alphabetise collection of pornography
10. Record continuous six-hour Trance mix (interrupted by toast and Marmite from Mum)

24

DEVIL'S DANDRUFF

● Hot Dog Merchant *Cheapus Meatus*

Most commonly found inhabiting areas heavily populated by minicab touts (*Drivus Badlyae*) and inebriated youngsters. Often drawn towards vomit-covered pavements, a good indication of opportunities for the mammal's primary objective: the selling of undercooked meat-like sausages and burnt onions to intoxicated men (*Lecherous Maximus*) who have failed to find a mate for the evening. Although slow (the symbiotic relationship with the *Trolley Rusticus* hampers any fast travelling speeds) the *Cheapus Meatus* is highly mobile and able to turn up at a gathering of drunken people within minutes. Years of exposure to stale meat has enabled the mammal to build up a unique genetic structure, one fully resistant to any form of food poisoning. As a result it shows a flagrant disregard for sell-by dates and hygiene laws.

Ill-fitting leather jacket

Yellow flavour sauce

Cooking knife

Bread

Special onion grease acne

Stabbing knife (hidden in trolley)

Other Late Night Snack Options

● **Pasties and rolls:**
Friendly, healthy looking packaging disguises the fact that most of these products contain exactly the same ratio of minced rats noses, cow hoofs and horse lips as a street hotdog.

● **Crisps:**
After hours any outlets left open only seem to stock special 'Grab Bag' size –same amount of crisps but bigger packet and twice the price.

● **Cheese Strings:**
For the more gourmand late night snacker these chewy plastic dairy by products are frequently a popular choice.

COMMUNICATION

Unlike most mammalia, the *Cheapus Meatus* enjoys a limited vocabulary, usually restricted to the following phrases:

★ 'Hot dog, hot dog'
★ 'Two pounds, chief'
★ 'You need minicab?'
★ 'I can get you other stuff'
★ 'Go see my man over there'

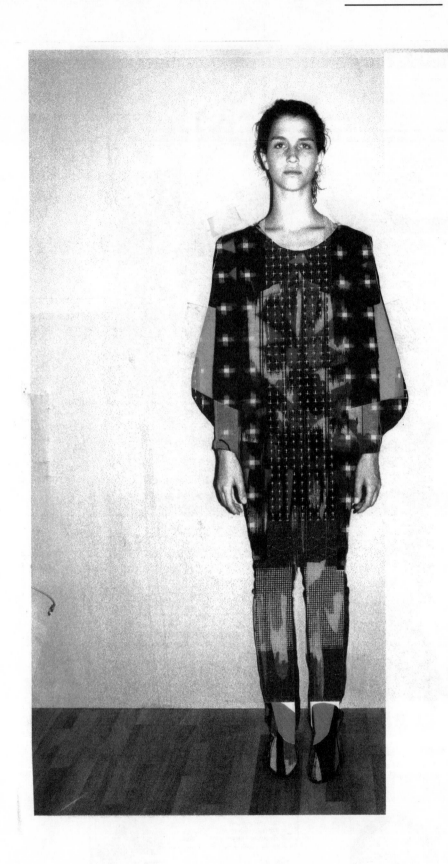

MARIE O'CONNOR
Archive
Textile Collection
2011
Found textile designs were multiplied,
inverted and manipulated using the
standard actions in Photoshop to create
multi-layered prints. In doing this, I tried
to create something new from old; the
garments themselves becoming an
archive of sorts while continuing to
re-invent themselves.

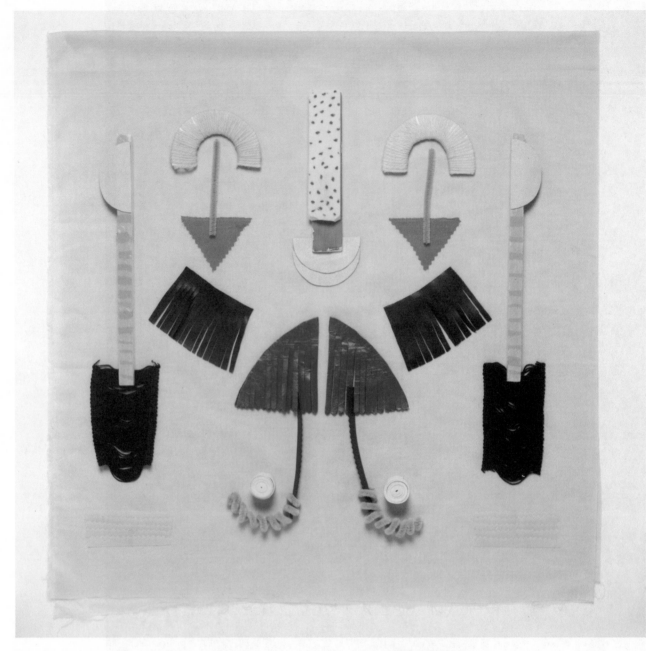

MARIE O'CONNOR
Totem
2010
Mixed media collage

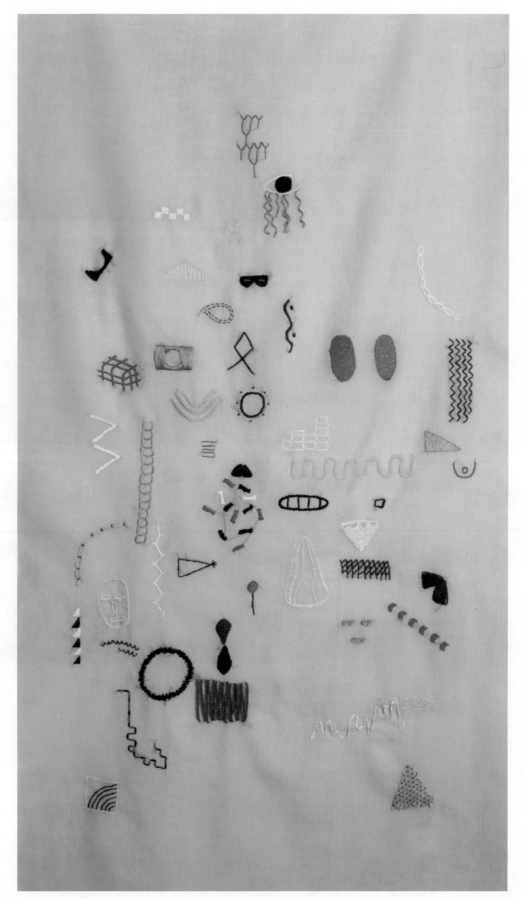

MARIE O'CONNOR
And what will all of this
become if not you?
2011
Stitch

PETE MELLOR (Director)
Cowards (12 x 2')
AngelEye/BBC
2007–2008

When working on comedy scripts, we try to elicit humour by showing certain aspects of a narration or voice-over without simply illustrating exactly what is being said. For the BBC4 comedy show Cowards, we kept the main scene very simple while using the cutaway to create a visual punchline – such as showing simple black and white versions of Harrison Ford's film biography while he is at a job interview or an empty park where everyone had supposedly agreed to meet Martin Clunes to play football.

'Polish Airmen' (2'45")
from the film 'A Liar's Autobigraphy'
Bill and Ben Productions
2011

For A Liar's Autobiography – the animated feature film based on the memoir of Monty Python star Graham Chapman – the challenge was how to visually interpret the absurdist script without getting in the way of the narration. The simple answer was that, where the script was over-the-top and silly, we would be restrained and not do too much and where the script was more straight-forward story-telling, we would go as far as we could – so we ended up including a decapitated head being used as a tea-pot.

ANDREW RAE (Director)
MTV Asia On Air Identity
2005
Animation: Luke Best, Robert Grieves,
Andrew Rae, Russ Murphy
Executive Producer: Charmaine Choo
This project had a self-deprecating
brief asking us to make light of the fact
that MTV viewers tend to switch over
once a music video finishes. For the
Idents I invented a cast of performing
characters desperately trying to
impress and hold on to the audience
but failing: the characters variously
fell over, fell asleep, were crushed or
sank. I flew out and spent a week in
Singapore, Malayasia and Penang with
tour guides showing me around while I
took notes and sketched, collected and
generally documented. I was struck by
the pace of progress so I made an ident
for a section called 'Now And Then', in
which an old Malay man is listening to
a Heath Robinson-style gramophone
and is suddenly crushed by a high-rise
building dropped in place by a crane.

Next page:
ANDREW RAE (Director)
The Stunt (3')
Mesh/Channel 4
Blackwatch Productions
2006
Animation: Luke Best, Pete Mellor,
Andrew Rae
In 2005 I entered a script into the Mesh
animation scheme and it was accepted.
The scheme included scriptwriting
workshops and funding to make a short
film, which was screened on Channel
4 in 2006. Technically, I was interested
in combining stop-framed handmade
models created by Chrissie and myself
with scenery and 2D animation done
in the computer. With hindsight I think
I tried to fit too much plot into the time
available but I'm happy with the look
and feel of the animation.

0.00.06.21

0.00.12.22

0.00.16.10

0.00.28.21

0.00.32.19

0.00.38.16

0.00.39.03

0.00.43.19

0.00.45.06

0.00.48.23

0.01.01.10

0.01.03.09

0.01.08.12

0.01.13.21

0.01.20.05

0.01.22.17

0.01.29.01

0.01.30.18

0.01.37.08

0.01.40.13

0.01.43.11

0.02.01.08

0.02.06.05

0.02.08.16

0.02.09.15

0.02.10.21

0.02.14.21

0.02.18.23

0.02.20.22

0.02.22.02

0.02.22.15

0.02.25.19

0.02.34.14

0.02.35.14

0.02.37.19

0.02.44.21

0.02.46.05

0.02.48.19

0.02.52.04

0.02.54.22

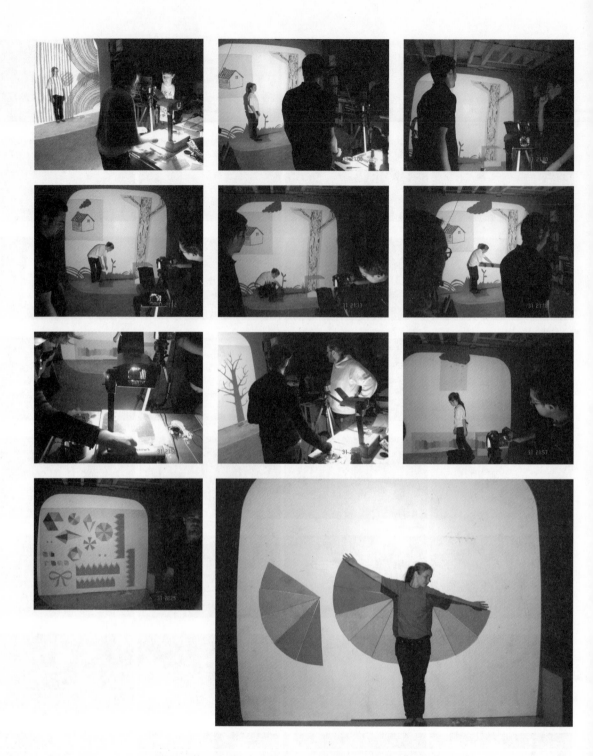

PEEPSHOW (Director)
counter_vision
onedotzero / The Hayward Gallery
2006

PEEPSHOW (Director)
Peepshow Animate the V&A
Victoria & Albert Museum /
Friday Late
2009
To coincide with the show Undercover
Surrealism at the Hayward, we were
invited by onedotzero to create a
piece of moving image for the event
counter_vision.

　Using the height of technology –
an overhead projector – some acetates
and a friend, we tried to create an
interplay between the real and the
projected. The girl moves through
patterns and landscapes, chops down
trees, creates a colour wheel and owns
many changing faces. The film was
shot frame by frame in our studio, with
the directions 'left a bit, up a bit', and
shown during an evening of films and
live performances that also featured
Black Convoy, New and Pandemonium.

　We used the same method for the
workshop at the V&A Friday Late with
the catchy title Peepshow Animate
the V&A.

　We asked the public to come
along and work with drawings of our
favourite things in the V&A archive.
Playing with these on the OHP, they
then had the opportunity to direct and
star in their own animation, appearing
alongside jangly skeletons, patterned
pottery and scary bunny rabbits.

Antarctic Expedition
DDB, London
2007
In the winter of 2007, we transformed
the reception of advertising agency
DDB London into 'Peepshow's Antarctic
Expedition'. The installation followed
a polar explorer across the Antarctic
landscape to his campsite. In the
street-level, double-height lobby we
constructed a faceted cliff face with
the explorer's base camp perched on
an ice ledge, his climbing ropes leading
up to the main reception area on the
first floor. Reception seating was
provided in the guise of a heavily laden
sledge; boxes stuffed with rations, the
explorers hand-drawn observation
notebooks and even hand-stitched
woollen socks and mittens. The project
was rounded off with the production of
DDB's animated Christmas card, which
explored the same snowy wilderness
as the installation.

polar bear
follows footsteps

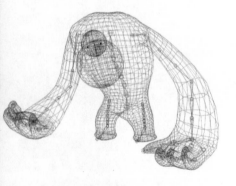

PETE MELLOR (Director)
Secret Santa (1'30")
DDB
2007

As an extension of the installation at DDB, we created an animation to be shown in the foyer and also used as an email-able Christmas card. We took the opportunity to continue the narrative from the installation further and show what was in the gift boxes. For this film we used some new techniques and on this occasion the challenge for me was to mix CGI characters with the more traditional hand-drawn and hand-cut background elements.

gift in trees

polar bear on ice floe

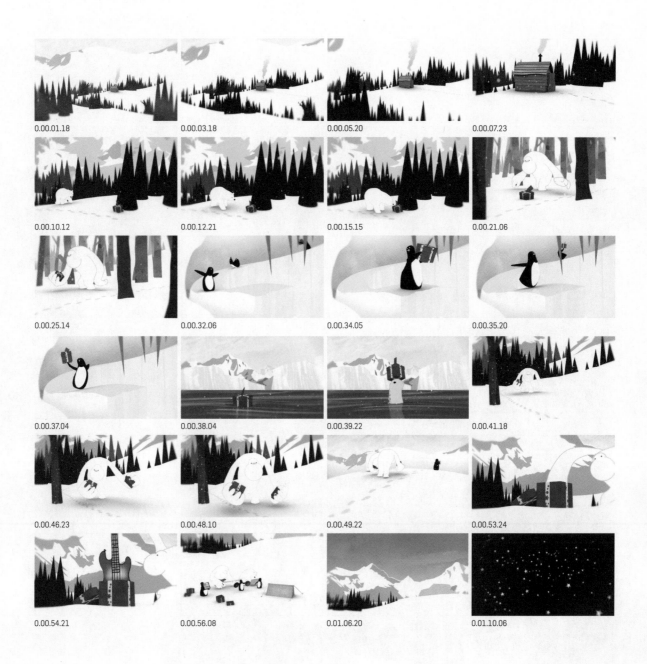

0.00.01.18   0.00.03.18   0.00.05.20   0.00.07.23

0.00.10.12   0.00.12.21   0.00.15.15   0.00.21.06

0.00.25.14   0.00.32.06   0.00.34.05   0.00.35.20

0.00.37.04   0.00.38.04   0.00.39.22   0.00.41.18

0.00.46.23   0.00.48.10   0.00.49.22   0.00.53.24

0.00.54.21   0.00.56.08   0.01.06.20   0.01.10.06

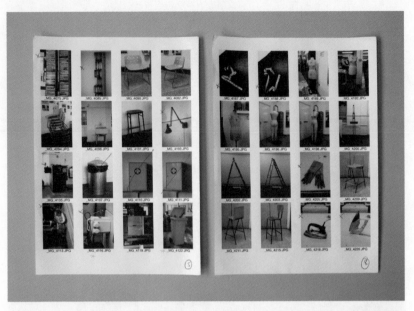

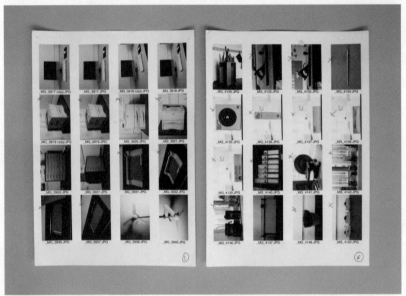

CHRISSIE MACDONALD
**Central Saint Martin's College
of Art and Design**
Poster and prospectus imagery
2008
Design & Art Direction: Praline
Photography: John Short
These compositions were created with
photographs of interiors, students,
materials and equipment from a broad
range of disciplines, combined in small
table-top sets to illustrate the diversity
of the courses on offer.

SPENCER WILSON
Let's Read Together
2011

What's the Time
2011

SPENCER WILSON
The Weather
theWeather Magazine
2010–2011
It's nice when a designer lets you work in a way that does not exist in your folio. This is the case with working for Mike at Em-Project. Having accepted the commission these editorials have energised my work and I've learnt a little about weather systems, volcanoes and snow rolls to boot.

LUCY VIGRASS
The People Who Couldn't Say
2005

In 2005 we had a show at 17 Gallery in Shoreditch, London. We have always had the policy of creating new artwork for our shows so I used this opportunity to create a series of images based on the lyrics of a song by Granddaddy about office workers winning a trip to the countryside. The narrative in the song suggested a jarring of the natural world and the man-made as the office workers struggled to quantify their new surroundings – leading to a protractor measuring the perpendicular nature of a tree, paper-clipping the leaves back onto trees and a desk lamp attracting moths at night.

LUCY VIGRASS
Catalyst
The Prince's Foundation for Children
and the Arts
Studio EMMI
2010

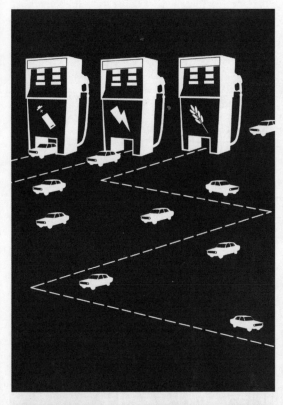

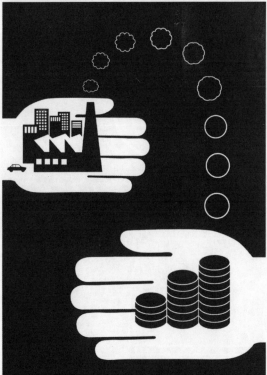
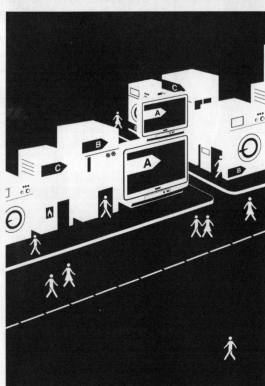

LUCY VIGRASS
In The Black: The growth of the Low
Carbon Economy summary report
Climate Group / Browns, London
2007

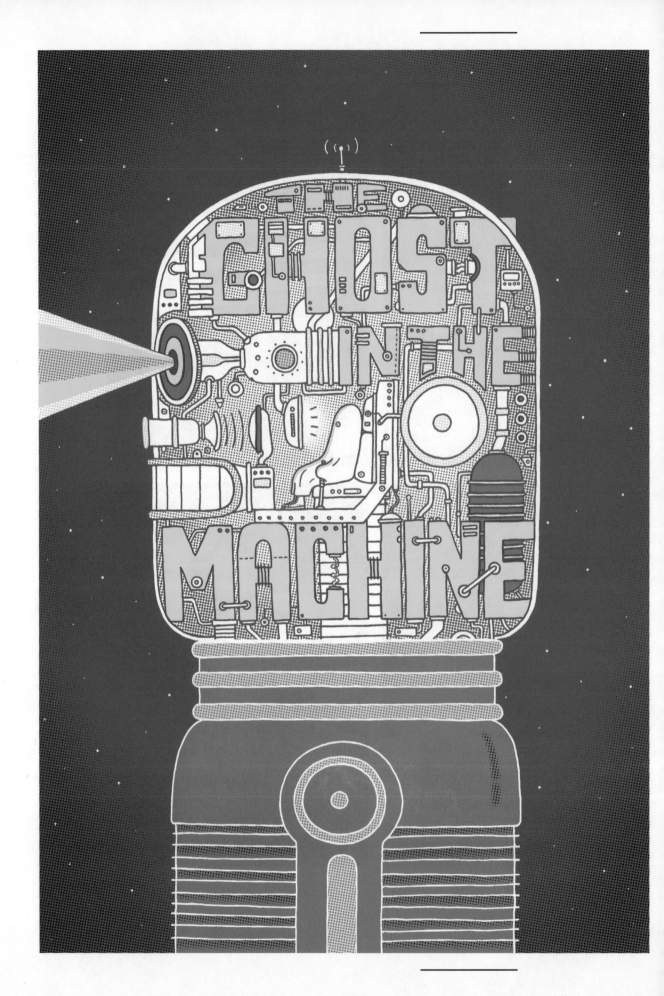

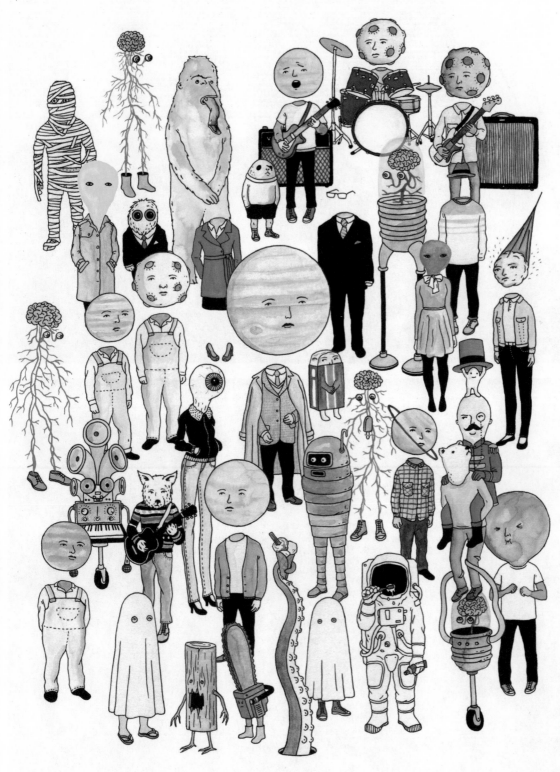

ANDREW RAE
Ghost in the Machine
Limited Edition Screen Print
2010

Moon Heads
Limited Edition Print produced
by Artspace
2011

ANDREW RAE
Monkey Dust
Talkback Thames
2002–2004
Mic Graves, the Creative Director, got
me in after seeing my work on a flyer
in a dark corner of a record shop. I
worked in-house at Talkback Thames
and I got very starstruck seeing Steve
Coogan, Armando Iannucci and Chris
Morris kicking around the building. It
was a dark satirical sketch show, which
required characters and scenery to be
created very quickly so the sketches
were farmed out to lots of animation
houses including Sherbet Animation,
Slinky Pictures and Nexus productions.
I was called designer and art director
at different times during the process
and my role was to create characters
and scenery and to create a look, feel
and colour scheme that could loosely
hold the different animators' styles
and ways of working together. It was a
great show and a fantastic project for
a young illustrator to cut his teeth on.
Sadly Harry Thompson, the maverick
producer and creative force behind the
show, died in 2005 and the television
landscape is a worse place for it.

HEAVY PENCIL

LIVE ART

LIVE MUSIC

THURS 17TH MARCH
JAMES JARVIS, WILL SWEENEY
ANDREW RAE, JIM STOTEN
LUKE BEST, NICK WHITE
GAVIN LUCAS, CHIEF CHUCKAROO

THURS 24TH MARCH
JIGGERY POKERY, JESS BONHAM
CHRISSIE MACDONALD, BEN FRY
ANDREW RAE, JIM STOTEN
CURLY STEVE, NICK WHITE

AT PICK ME UP SOMERSET HOUSE
6-9 PM, ENTRANCE INCLUDED IN FAIR TICKET £7/£5, WWW.SOMERSETHOUSE.ORG.UK/PICKMEUP

AT SOMERSET HOUSE

 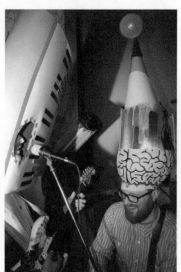 

Heavy Pencil East
2009–2011
Heavy Pencil was created by Gemma Tortella as a live drawing event at the ICA – she asked Andrew and Luke to take part in March 2009. Subsequently she let us take on the name and put on more Heavy Pencil nights with live music in East London at Catch 22 bar and at Pick Me Up at Somerset House. These events have featured live art and music from Jim Stoten, Nick White, James Jarvis, Will Sweeney, Jiggery Pokery, Al Murphy, Jess Bonham, Adrian Johnson and many more.

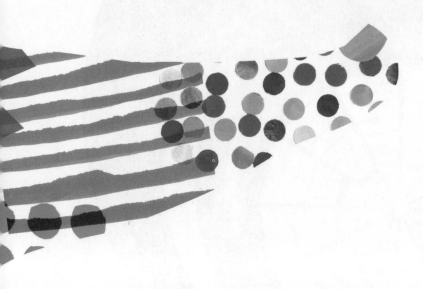

Previous spread:
JENNY BOWERS
Patterns
Roxy, Waitrose, Afternoon tea,
White Stuff
2006–2011
The patterns here are from various
commissions over the past five years.
I was lucky enough to be part of the
Roxy Studio, which comprised of
several artists and illustrators in the
UK and US who produced work for
Roxy for different seasons over two
and a half years. The brief was always
very open and it gave me a lot of room
to experiment with shape and colour,
producing designs in great volume.
The patterns were then collated and
applied to various products, labels
and even a Roxy bus.

Leaf
2005
This image was part of a set of paintings
of leaf shapes that I did one afternoon.
Not an awful lot of thought went into
the image and I think this is its success.
It feels spontaneous and I think this is
when my work, works best.

This page:
Feet
howies
2007
Clothing company howies has
commissioned me over the past
six years for their catalogue and it's
always a pleasure to work with them.

GUGGENHEIM MUSEUM

MILES DONOVAN
Guggenheim
2009

Sound in Print
2007

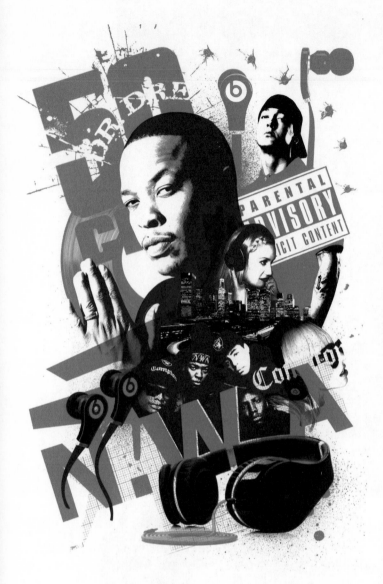

MILES DONOVAN
Dr Dre
The Guardian
2009

Technology
Icon Magazine
2008

ASOS
The Telegraph
2008
Around about 2006 I started to develop
a new way of working that allowed
me the freedom to work quite quickly
and crudely after years of meticulous
sprayed processes. This collage style
developed from a fast editorial cover
for The New York Times when I had two
days to complete five illustrations.

MILES DONOVAN
Rihanna
The Observer Music Monthly
2006

Kylie Minogue
The Observer Music Monthly
2007

Prince
The Observer Music Monthly
2005
Between 2005 and 2007, I completed
a monthly illustration for the Singles
Review section of The Observer Music
Monthly magazine. The portraits
included the likes of The Arctic
Monkeys, Girls Aloud and Missy Elliot
but it's the portraits of Kylie, Prince
and Rihanna that are my favourites.
I realised shortly after that I'd exhausted
the possibilities of ink and a limited
colour palette so started to develop
a new way of working, but it was
fun while it lasted and led to similar
commissions for Billboard, Defected
Records and ITV.

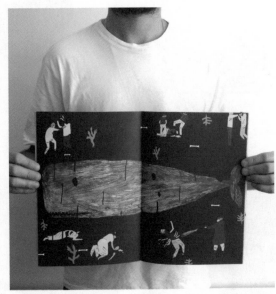

Whale kills trainer at theme park

By Fred Attewill

A KILLER whale fatally attacked a trainer at a theme park as horrified visitors looked on yesterday.

The mammal grabbed the woman around the waist and "thrashed her all around", according to a witness.

She had just finished explaining to the audience the show they were about to see when she slipped into the tank.

Paramedics were unable to revive the 40-year-old at Florida's SeaWorld Orlando, a theme park which is a popular destination for hundreds of thousands of British holidaymakers.

Describing the attack, park visitor Victoria Biniak said: "He was thrashing her around pretty good.

"One of the trainer's shoes fell off, it

was pretty violent." The park was evacuated and then closed following the incident.

There have been several previous attacks on whale trainers at SeaWorld parks.

In 2006, trainer Kenneth Peters was bitten and held underwater several times by a 5,175kg (7,000lb) killer whale during a show at SeaWorld's San Diego park. The 39-year-old escaped with a broken foot.

The 5m (17ft) long orca who attacked him was the dominant female of the park's seven killer whales. She had also attacked him in 1993 and 1999.

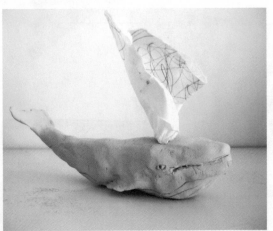

LUKE BEST
Whale cushions (front)
Curse of the Whale, Nobrow issue 3
Newspaper clipping
Clay model
Whale cushions (Back)
Lino and fabric scraps
2010

Overleaf:
Various elements
2011

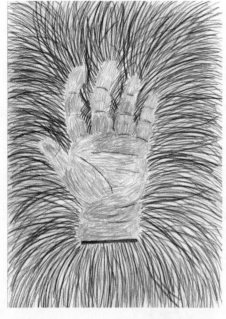

LUKE BEST
The Hand- a series of Pencil drawings
The Funeral Parlor
The Hand
The Coven
The Incinerator
The Nest
The Fountain
2009
coloured pencil
29.7cm x 21cm

While on a trip to Portland, I went to a reading by Katherine Dunn of her short story That's all I know (right now), based on the song with the same name by Sonic Youth. The story is about the discovery of a severed hand in a local park. The people of Portland speculate about the various origins of the hand and how it became separated from its owner. This sequence of drawings focuses on the gaps in the story, where the hand may have come from and the harsh truth of its existence. With the drawings I was trying to combine the said, physical aspects of the narrative with the imagined bits outside of the text. I wanted the images to be able to stand alone but ultimately work as a series. The drawings were later reworked, translating the pencil language to black ink, also extending the series in order to become a screen-printed publication by Nobrow.

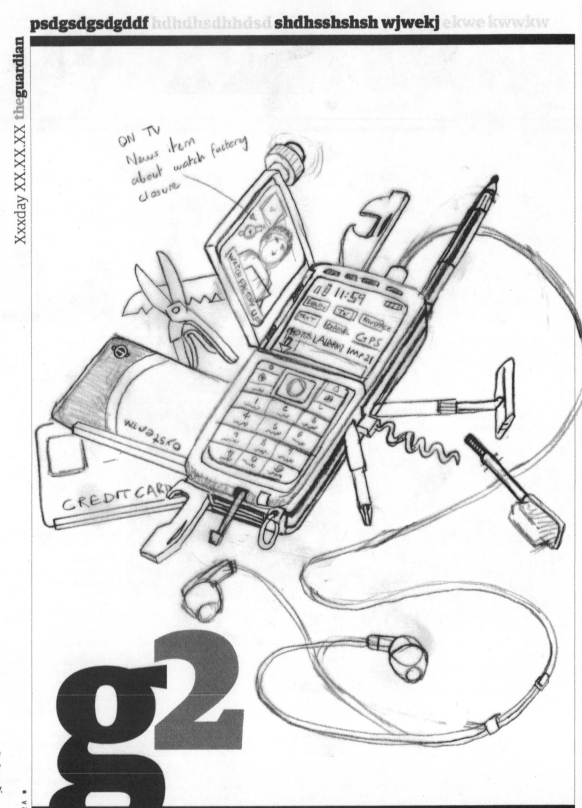

ELLIOT THOBURN
Future Mobile
Guardian G2
2007
The Swiss Army phone. This was the
client's idea, but it was a nice idea to
run with. The rough and the artwork
usually end up different in some way,
though on this occasion the rough
isn't far off the final version. The
G2's predictions about the future
of mobile phones were also pretty
close to the mark.

Thursday 08.03.07 **theguardian**

g2

**Goodbye camera,
watch, diary, radio,
iPod, laptop ...**

**What the do-it-all mobile
means for modern life**

ELLIOT THOBURN
Mark Webber's 'Dinners With'
Red Bulletin F1 Magazine
2008

Collin Kolle's 'Dinners With'
Red Bulletin F1 Magazine
2008
People from the world of F1 choose
their six ideal dinner guests. With
portraits finding a good set of
references is a must and those
references more often than not will
dictate the visual and conceptual
content of the final artwork. As for
Elliot Thoburn's 'dinners with'
Toshiro Mifune, Joe Strummer,
Eddie Izzard, Yasuko Matsuyuki,
Lauren Bacall and Inoue Takehiko
would be the guests.

*In one year,
a car can produce
4 times
its own weight in carbon dioxide.

be good, drive small

* http://www.wycombe.gov.uk/sitePages.asp?step=4&contentID=623&categoryID=321

SPENCER WILSON
Be Green
2008
When it goes quiet, the fear sets in.
'Will I ever be commissioned again?'
Everyone needs a driving force.
Fortunately I've had two great role
models in my parents and a high-
achieving sister to compete with. Be
Green was born out of a quiet time, I
like to respond to copy so I found some
facts from my friend the Internet and
just produced some visuals. I limited
the palette, introduced some textures.
Imagery happens in an accidental
way for me, sometimes it works and
sometimes it exists in bits on some
random art board titled 'Shit'.

AS EASY 1 2 3

SPENCER WILSON
Elements Artboard
2009–2011

SPENCER WILSON
A Brief History of Hybrid
Honda Dream Magazine
2010

Hydro Electricity – Cover image
Honda Dream Magazine
2009

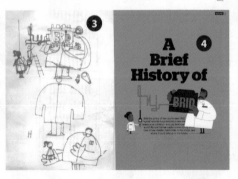

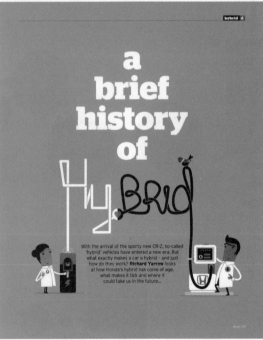

dream

the magazine for Honda customers

discover the world's cleanest car
meet three modern multi-taskers
drive the 2008 Honda S2000
win a designer eco-accessory

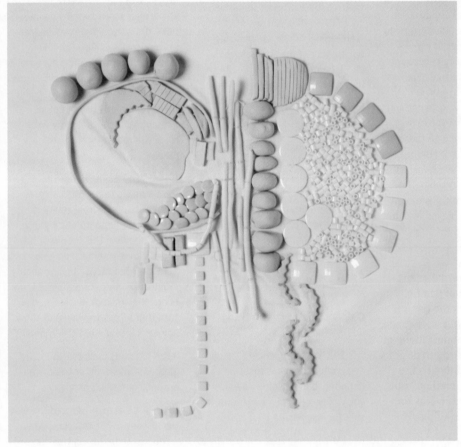

MARIE O'CONNOR
Clothing as Collage
Film and textile collection
2008
As I see it, the body is a mixed media, multi-layered object. The film and textiles explore embroidery and print as separate layers to the clothing base, moving around the body with a mind of their own. Elements from the original collages made when designing the garments are incorporated into the imagery in the film, playing with scale and inextricably linking the process to the final execution.

INTERVIEW Pt. 03
With Peter Nencini
Assisted by Freya Faulkner

PN: About the spaces in between you. Firstly the studio. In each incarnation, rather than opaque walls marking off individual workspaces, it seems you've done it with low box shelves of books and objects. Is this a direct or indirect resource for your work (given Google image search)? Is it there in a more ambient way, to make a stimulating environment; or as a 'library'?

LB: I think it's changed, in terms of its usage. It's still there but it operates slightly differently. I'd say it's more ambient now than it used to be. So it's more of a leftover. We all have less material but it's more specific, over time you are more sure of your interests and edit out what is less important to you.

JB: When I read your question last night, I had a look. I turned; spun around in my chair and I immediately saw my fabulous gold bar.

MD: That's been in every studio.

JB: It's just a piece of wood on which Lucy painted the word 'gold', which is brilliant. It says so many things! It makes me laugh and it makes me think about the old studio and it makes me think about the way we approach things.

MO: I don't have anything sentimental in my workspace at all – or anything that anyone's given to me. Sometimes I collect or keep things for that reason but they're usually at home, kind of displayed in a particular neurotic order. When I was in Peepshow's studio, in the first incarnation I remember (and I still do it now) that on the righthand side of my desk there was always a little sculptural 'thing'; a piece of paper with a blob of Plasticine. And I realise that when I'm sitting doing a piece of work, I'm also doing something on the side. I'm surrounded by objects, bits and offcuts. Sometimes they go directly go into the work as an object or a mark but other times they're just there on the periphery, the formal qualities slowly informing something. It's more about having something that makes you think you're on the right track. Having all those bits at my disposal but also not becoming anything yet; it makes me feel really comfortable. They can become the work or they can just be a thing I've played with for five minutes, then they're taken apart again.

PN: In other conversations, you've talked about what you've learnt from the person in the neighbouring workspace, in the various manifestations of the studio – not through direct collaboration, but just by the proximity of their method, tools, set-up, rhythm, habit. Can we discuss specific examples?

LV: With (sitting next to) Luke, it was just a freedom to 'do'; just to get on with it and play. And I don't really have that.

CM: You don't give yourself that?

LV: No. Well, it's just not in me, necessarily. Which is why I think I used to have a process that was quite random. Like, designing with Lego or something like that. I'm not very good at playing or mark-making and I think being next to Luke is… I don't know… it's nice to watch someone do something that's so completely at odds with the way you do it.

LB: I'd say in response to that: what's good about those things is that maybe it affirms something in yourself, in that you see me doing it and think: "It looks enjoyable but that's not me and not what I do." In your work I appreciate the logic; the system that's happening and how you're making an image. I know I can't do that well. The same with everyone. You can appreciate what someone is doing but actually it helps you reaffirm your own philosophy behind the work. If you did try and step into that other person's shoes you realise that it's uncomfortable and not where your interests lie. I find that really good, across the board.

SW: I sat opposite Miles, when Miles had a quiff.

CM: And you started drawing quiffs. (laughter).

AR: But I'd say Spencer's colour and composition has most definitely been inspiring because you've always had a very natural skill for composition.

LV: I also found that being in a room and having somebody – not quite looking over your shoulder, but there – pushes you harder and stops you being lazy. I don't just want to sit there and 'bosh' something out because I'll feel embarrassed about it.

AR: And you'd be more embarrassed about what everyone else in the room thinks of it than the art director does.

LV: I want to live up to what everyone else is doing; definitely.

ET: I've never been part of the studio, I'm fully aware of how easily distracted I am by people, but I did work alongside Spencer at Southwark College and his constant desire to adapt his work is something which rubbed off on me. He did influence me into changing my style and my use of colour. Although conceptually my work is very much the same beast it's always been.

LB: Also, working alongside Pete – he's a really good animator – but actually his real talent is in direction and how to tell a story by not showing the action. Or how sound can say something else. That's helped me. If I think about illustration, sometimes I will think about the ambient noise; I can turn that into a drawing and show something that's not the 'moment'.

AR: That goes back to the 'pregnant moment' or the moment around something happening.

SW: Pete's also influenced the way that I pose my characters. When he makes them move, they have a certain weight about them that makes me know how they're going to fall. That's come straight into my work.

PN: In direct collaboration with another, how has your work – practically, conceptually – been affected? In the sense that, when two of you work together, a 'third' thing comes out. How did this fold back into your longer term practice?

AR: That's happening to me right now. I'm working on this film – with Pete – which is a Monty Python feature. It's the story of Graham Chapman. In order to make the animation work, we decided to lose the line. All my work is, basically, about line. So, to drop the line has felt quite drastic. It's been a really interesting process and it works well in animation because you can describe the shape of something so much more. Well, it gives it more ambiguity.

LV: Without any lines to explain the form you really have to get the shape right. Otherwise it can look really odd or misshapen. The silhouette becomes so important.

AR: Yes, especially when it's moving, there's a lot of form and weight that wouldn't be there, so that might work its way into my work in the future. It's something I'd been toying with anyway. That's one of those things where it's hard to persuade a client: "I'm going to do it like this; it's nothing like any work I've ever done."

MD: When we pitched for CBeebies, I think it's the first time that we all just came to the table with lots of ideas and drawings and amalgamated the bits we liked and came out with something different that not one single person would come up with.

CM: I learnt I have a tendency to go too clean and polished and tasteful – which are the things I don't like about my work. Working with Marie on If You Could: Collaborate, I learnt that you can do something that's a bit 'off', or that you can use a colour you don't instinctively go for. Or, leaving something not quite perfect; but that gives it a charm.

PN: I remember coming to see you two, when you were just at the beginning of that process. Once when you had started to make table-sized models for one another and then, when you'd moved next door and acquired, temporarily, another space. You were staring at lots of human-sized pieces of wood and salvage. Kind of happily bewildered about what you were going to do next. It was as if the whole methodology had to be considered. As if a third person had entered the room and said: "We're going to do…"

CM: I think it was also a case of both of us deciding what we wanted to do more of but weren't necessarily doing. We both had the desire to work bigger and wanted to work with wood. So it was things we'd been thinking about and If You Could gave us the chance to do it.

MO: There was a moment where – because our references are similar and we had similar ideas to make something big or in a robust material – when we'd moved into that room and we had all of those things, there was lots of dialogue but lots of making. Making, a bit, because we didn't know what else to do. Which you'd said you'd enjoyed because it was just playing. That's the way that I work quite naturally, so I was thinking: "Oh, what's this going to become?" So, although we had a shared idea of what we were doing, it was kind of twisted on both parts. I really liked laying the materials out in the space. So that they weren't going to become figures; they were just colours, or textures. And that's a crucial point. In my head at that moment it could have become something 'else' and I know in your head, it could have become completely different as well. So then, we had to go back to the original idea of a kit of parts and not introducing too many other elements; working purely with what we had and still going for the figures. That was the thing driving us, in a way.

AR: You were also a little scared of stealing each other's identities. When it does cross over too much, you ask: "Is that mine now? Am I allowed to use that?"

MO: One person can really get into something and have a vision for how to follow it through. Although the other person appreciates that, it might not necessarily be how the two should take it.

LB: Collaboration works well when no-one has the identity in it. When it was the stall with the vegetables (for V&A Village Fête), we had other roles and skills that aren't to do with our work but how we operate as a collective, in terms of organising and building,

or being the stallholder. It's another side of how we operate. It isn't about the making of the work but about setting up the moment for something to happen. I think that's when we work at our best as a group.

LV: We're all quite satellite. We're not such an homogenous group. We're all, quite defiantly, individual. Actually we're a nightmare to collaborate with (laughs), because we're all strong-minded about what we want to do and how we want to do it.

JB: But we know that.

PN: About the space around you. Can we talk about processes which orbit your illustration, design, animation process? Or those that sit parallel? Activity that, laterally, indirectly, nourishes what you do. You (Andrew), with your music, for example.

AR: I've always made a direct correlation between the process of making music and of making images, in that it's about practice – which is something you have to do as a musician – and then, a performance, which is the drawing. Then, the recording process, which is where the computer comes in.

LB: And how it's received? In terms of the way music – or a drawing – communicates?

AR: I think they're very different. I mean, it's partly why I started drawing in front of people, because it's just the pressure of having to do it. Just having the 'chops'. I like the challenge; and I like the fear of it.

LB: The Heavy Pencil events are good, because it's not prescribed drawing but just trying to respond to the music. I enjoy it because an important part of my process is just trying to be uncomfortable.

AR: With drawing you're always in that state of not knowing if it's going to work.

SW: For me to pick up a pencil and paint, then that's a complete fear set. But once you overcome it, then it's easier isn't it? At the minute, my drawing's easy, illustration-wise, because I know the rules. And every once in a while I add a new rule: I might put a nose in, or feet...

MD: This is where Spenny steps out of his box (laughter).

AR: I prefer to draw as practice.

LB: Your drawing and your drawing for illustration are quite closely matched. They really inform each other. I have moments of drawing that don't directly inform my illustration work. I do have an interest in drawing but drawing for illustration is of a certain type I think, and it only expands so far, whereas drawing in art practice is much more open. So there's a crossover.

PN: Heavy Pencil is interesting because as a form, it's quite new – if I think about graffiti – but the side of it which is about somebody who is a content-based image-maker making, or 'scribing' content live to an audience, so you're speaking to them and doing so instantaneously – there's some form there which could be applied in other ways. It's when something is done that feels like it's on the side and it's an amalgamation of your love of performance, music and illustration – but then it genuinely suggests another kind of form.

AR: I do feel like it could go somewhere. I'm not sure where that is but I do think it could be a different form in some way. I like the idea of just being able to get ideas across quickly.

PN: You've talked to me previously in a quite abstract way about your music. I mean, reaching for something. It's interesting if that, then, can stretch the way you think about your illustration work, even if a client isn't asking you to think about it in that way. It gives it an extra dimension; having a conversation with yourself about what you're doing.

AR: I think that's how I'm thinking about my drawing at the moment, which is very different to the way I used to think about it like a 'gag', or an image that you get straight away; which is why it could be applied to advertising quite easily. I'm now definitely interested in it becoming more ambiguous. More of a language.

MD: Does your allotment feed into your work, Spenny?

SW: It just takes me to another place. I like going there. It's nature; the birds are there; I can build stuff with wood; I can grow and just be in a different zone.

PN: Does it come from the same energy point as your work here?

SW: The energies have just started coming back. Where I'm at now: I've just started to feel like I'm more in control of what I want to be doing with my work and also not just working all the time. In an ideal world, it would be one day printing, one day allotment and perhaps two days' illustration.

I do have to think: "What are my interests?" My wife's a primary school teacher and my kids probably feed into my work practice more than I credit. I've started to become more interested in kids' illustrated books and producing images that are a lot 'younger'. And hopefully that then gets the commissions in, that pays the money, that keeps me happy, that allows me to go to the allotment, to grow stuff and build stuff and be a bit more creative.

JB: I've always enjoyed making things – whatever they might be – out of fabric, painting, cardboard boxes, whatever. I was wanting to say a bit earlier, about the extra projects that we do that are not commissioned work, like the Pick Me Up (printing workshop) thing – I think it's so liberating and that's what makes me make work that I really enjoy.

PN: Jenny, looking at your work. Having a child now – that way that they re-teach you how to work quickly or to enjoy materials – you can definitely see how that is beneficial. The… breeziness. The caring about not caring too much or the use of accident; or the way that you cut. It's important, it seems, for the freshness and vitality of the work.

JB: That's pretty much how I work and how I make. I have a very short space of time and I have to just sit and do it.

PN: Do you think that's to its benefit?

JB: Yeah, I would say.

LB: You still make that selection though, don't you, where you'll make ten really quick brushmarks and then choose from those which one's right? So it still has that breeziness but it's not off-the-cuff.

JB: And when I get commissioned, what they want: that lightness and immediacy. I'm really desperate to do something that has a bit more longevity.

CM: Going the other way, I spend too long doing everything, so that process of doing something quick and rough, I'm really enjoying.

SW: I aspire to that. To be able to just make one mark.

MO: A little bit like Jenny doing stuff for her son Ed, I think teaching is a way to step outside yourself. All the obvious things. To be part of a creative dialogue but also to even think about solutions to being stuck. I did the workshop with primary school kids (for ReachOut RCA) and that was really interesting because they did what I expected them to do but also other things, over and above. Whether that's a communication thing or just their understanding of what they wanted to do. Just thinking about learning really.

I also think that teaching is my work. In a very literal sense, I research and I deliver things and I talk to people. It's enriching for your own brain and practice. Also, I give it as much time or more

time, usually, within my practice. Workshop-based teaching is an extension of this and – for the Royal College – that's what they wanted it to be – kind of boiling down how I work and imparting that to ten year-olds. I just find it interesting: a pedagogical approach to making.

ET: Teaching really fed all parts of my creative process and I very much miss the effect it had on me. The real thing that I enjoy conceptually is social commentary and in that respect the thing which fuels my ideas and still motivates me is living in the city. The stress, the drive, the frustration and the huge melting pots that are London and Tokyo: though they are two very different entities, they are both a constant source of inspiration.

MO: Everything that goes into the working process is important to us all. In some way you're always 'switched on'; I think it embellishes not just the work but the person. It seems the weight of everyone's reference, or childhood, or what they listen to, or whatever that source material is, gets channelled into work.

AR: But 'work' is the wrong word. It should be 'play'. When you make music, you call it *playing* an instrument. It should be the same when you make a drawing. *Playing* a drawing. It shouldn't be called 'work'.

PN: As an entity – in what you've done and the space you've occupied – do ou think you've helped to change the rules? A paradigm shift in illustration practice?

Or the way students might understand the industry they are going into, by looking at you and what you do?

LV: I think we've shown the benefit of sticking together as a group; and doing it yourself.

MD: Maybe the idea that you don't just have to sit and draw pictures. Whether it's art direction, styling, or animation; we've always had a go. So if you're offered something, you tend to accept it, try it and see what the outcome is.

LV: Whenever we've given talks, it seems to me the thing that students have been most excited about is the fact that we've stuck together and that 'have-a-go' mentality. It blows a myth away.

MO: I think that myth… I think it's difficult to blow your own trumpet. But maybe I could try to blow it (laughter). In many ways, I feel like an outsider because I'm not an illustrator per se and not ex-Brighton and don't have a space in the studio any more; I'm in a completely different place most of the time. But I do think that Peepshow are really visible. Not only in students' work – the way people have images of everyone's work in sketchbooks, talking about them or the level of interest when there's been talks – but just in a kind of mentality or attitude.

It's going back to the very first question, which was about those illustration annuals – that you realised illustration was there as an industry – but you never really tuned into it, until certain people came up. I think Peepshow's quite unique in the sense that everyone has got a strong client list and is prolific individually, without changing... It's apparent from this conversation that everyone has a belief in what they do and constantly want to learn, change, collaborate and grow. Prolific - individually and also as a group - it's not within a room, where everybody's in a kind of sycophantic group; it's actually taken out to an event, or an institution; out in the world somehow. It's being brave or inquisitive enough to do something in the V&A, Hayward, Somerset House. I think the evidence is there. If you look at people's track records – their commercial and personal work – it does mean something. Maybe it doesn't to the person in the street but within the industry maybe...

PN: It's also coincided with more people wanting to study illustration. And, in a not so fortunate way, 'illustration' as a kind of lifestyle. Do you think that there's been any effect on the form itself? On the discipline? Of doing illustration? I mean, in the work you've done. The fact that there's a strength in a number of people having a shared ethic. And so on.

MO: The discipline is seen in more contexts. More applications.

LB: There's a high level of our work that is applied. We're not a collective making really exciting work that is just for our own benefit and dismissing what we do for a living. All the stuff we're putting out – most of it in this book – is applied, commercial work, because we think we can do that to a high standard.

JB: The thing that people latch onto is that we somehow manage to keep a spirit of 'college'. Maybe what's new is that we are a company but in an informal way. There are a lot more collectives now than there were. And I don't know whether we helped people to do that.

CM: Or was that naturally going to happen anyway?

PN: So, does it make business sense for you to be a collective? Is that a business model?

AR: In the past, we've had discussions about making it into an agency, or becoming more of a 'business'; but we always pull back from that.

MD: But we couldn't operate the way we go about projects now without being a business and having a joint bank account. We got to the point in the old studio in Bethnal Green where we were dipping into our pockets every five minutes, to build a pot of money in order to do something. It just doesn't make sense.

LV: Again, it comes down to the fact that we're all quite individual. We've tried several things but we're so individual that it will never be anything other that what it is. I don't mean that in a sad way. It's just the conclusion we've come to. It's just what we've learnt. It is what it is.

NEW

The following nine spreads show
individual work created with
a limited palette exclusively
for this book.

LUKE BEST

LUCY VIGRASS

MARIE O'CONNOR

SPENCER WILSON

ELLIOT THOBURN

JENNY BOWERS

ANDREW RAE

MILES DONOVAN

CHRISSIE MACDONALD in
collaboration with Andrew Rae

TWO WILL

BECOME

A

STAMPEDE

ROARING

RAGING

TOWARDS A

NEW LAND

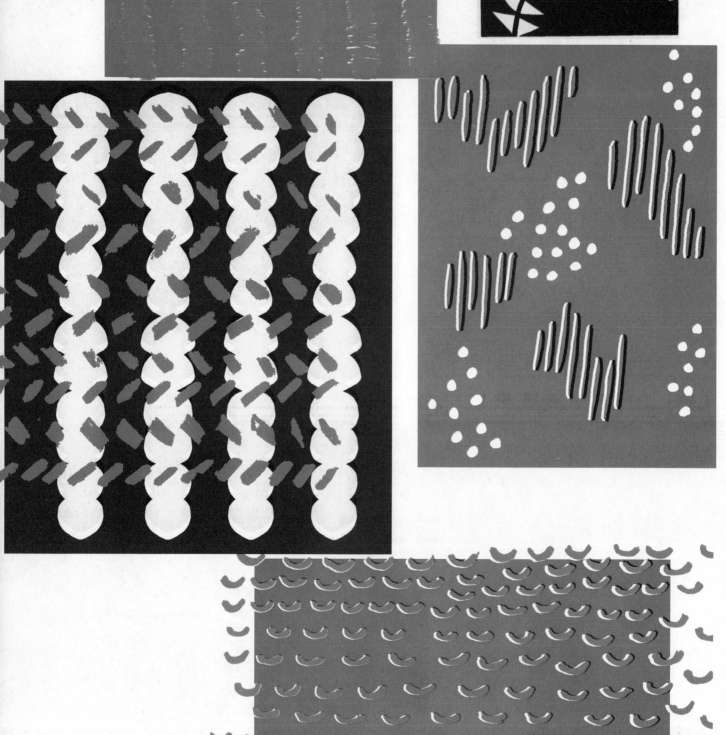

TIMELINE

1985 ⌄
Jenny & Lucy meet on their first day at Middle school.

1993 ⌄
Luke & Chrissie meet on the BTEC Art & Design course at Richmond College.

1995 ⌄
Future Peepshow founders meet on induction day at Brighton University – everyone presents their summer project self-portrait. Pete produces a nude portrait with modesty covered by guitar. Pete thinks this is funny. Everyone else thinks 'Who is this weirdo?'.

1997 ⌄
Jenny graduates from Manchester Metropolitan University with BA in Illustration and Animation and moves to London to go to RCA.

1998 ⌄
Spencer & Miles apply to the MA communication course at the RCA but don't get in. Their joint portfolio, a large hand built shipping crate taped to a skateboard leads to a new regulation for application the following year... NO large joint portfolios.

Chrissie, Miles, Andrew, Spencer, Pete, Lucy, Graham & Chris graduate from The University of Brighton with a BA (Hons) in Illustration.

Jenny graduates from RCA with MA in Animation. Gets first animation commission making interstitials for Channel 4 animation show 'Dope Sheet'.

Luke graduates from the illustration course at Brighton and starts MA at RCA

Andrew commissioned by BBH for a Lynx deodorant campaign.

Spencer starts working for a gold mining company and acquires an excellent grounding in Nigerian accounts policy of paying in 190 days.

Lucy's first commission for Pil Magazine.

Andrew's first commission; a cartoon for Tatler. They didn't use it.

Chrissie's first commission; 'I'm a Model' fashion story for Sleazenation magazine, featuring cut-out photographic figures of future Peepshow members.

1999 ⌃
Miles starts teaching on his old art foundation course in Maidenhead, Berkshire, three years after leaving as a student.

Spencer starts work as a legal messenger dropping his illustration portfolio off en route around London.

Miles' first commission is a record sleeve for R&B act 'Sneekie & Toyboy'. It is their first and last single.

Marie graduates from Glasgow School of Art with a degree in Embroidered & Woven Textiles.

Miles works at music store 'Our Price'. Serves Orbital and Tracey Emin.

Spencer starts work as a print technician at Southwark college.

Spencer's first paid commission for St. Lukes.

Miles & Lucy are approached by artist and writer Graham Rawle to act as assistants on a huge installation at Expo 2000 in Hanover, Germany. Andrew, Chrissie, Graham, Chris and Jenny are also soon involved.

2000 ⌄
Pete graduates from Royal College of Art with an MA in Animation and begins work as a production and post-production runner in Soho, London. He also begins freelance animation work at design and production company INTRO.

Lucy & Graham Carter run a newsagent in Elephant and Castle. Lucy headhunted Graham from Harvey Nichols, ladies vestments.

Marie starts a months placement with fashion label 'i.e uniform' in London. She ends up staying for over a year.

Jenny directs first and last animated music promo for Big Dada records.

Jenny realises animation is maybe not really her thing afterall.

A meeting is held in a pub in Tooting, South London, 'Peepshow Collective' is formed.

Elliot's first illustration commission for a marketing company in Brighton. Also starts teaching at Southwark College, alongside Spencer.

Andrew starts doing monthly flyers for Perverted Science.

Andrew gets a full time job as a web designer. Dot com bubble bursts and he's made redundant within the first three months. Does various odd jobs to pay the rent. Works at HM Prison Service entering data and at the Dome in charge of the bouncy castle.

Marie signs with Creative Union artist management. First illustration commissions follow for Levis, Tank and Dazed & Confused.

Elliot graduates from The University of Brighton with a BA (Hons) in Illustration.

Jenny starts working at the BBC as a production design assistant and misses the big trip to Expo in Germany, but she did visit Tate Modern on the day it opened instead.

2001

Lucy assists Graham Rawle in the creation of 'Niff Actuals'. Mainly paid in lovely lunches and 6 o'clock martinis.

Andrew invited to work on the first series of BBC's 'Monkey Dust'.

Luke's first commission for the Guardian Guide.

Marie goes out in East London. Carrying a portfolio is an obvious error/lucky charm. She meets Spencer and friends in a club.

The first Peepshow website designed by Andrew & Spencer is launched.

Chrissie works as art department assistant on the movie 'Thunderpants'. Andrew gets involved to design and man a flying machine. He is paid to shave off his beard.

 Luke graduates from RCA and hands out free newspapers at Bank train station. Forms directing duo with Luke Roszkowski 'Rosco and Best'.

2002

Elliot contributes to Shoreditch Twat magazine.

Miles' begins weekly illustrations for the Restaurant Review section of FT magazine. Quits working at 'Our Price'.

'Pen & Mouse' by Angus Hyland is published featuring the work of Miles, Lucy and Spencer.

Marie shows Peter Nencini her portfolio and begins teaching part time at Camberwell on the Communication Foundation course.

First Peepshow exhibition, New Inn Yard Gallery, Shoreditch, London.

Chrissie does a week long art department work placement on 'Harry Potter and the Chamber of Secrets'.

The first of many Tantramar nights at Hat on Wall in Clerkenwell with DJ's Miles, Stephen Lenthall and Charlie Gower. It's a regular Peepshow haunt for many years to come.

Peepshow exhibition tours St Lukes, M+C Saatchi & Ogilvy advertising agencies. We also take part in the London Artists Book Fair for the first time.

Marie, Luke, Elliot, Jenny & Duffy join Peepshow.

Chrissie works in the window display department at Harvey Nicols for a year.

Andrew starts teaching part time on the Foundation at Camberwell College.

2003

2nd series of 'Monkey Dust', Andrew works in-house at Talkback. Promoted to Art Director.

'Perverted Science' exhibition at Dreambagsjaguarshoes in East London.

'Humans vs The Robots' show in Farringdon featuring the work of Marie, Pete, Spencer & Andrew.

Luke starts teaching part time.

Elliot illustrates Observer Music Monthly column which runs for two years – and starts 333 flyers.

2004

Devil's Dandruff Column in the Guardian Guide starts, illustrated by Elliot.

The first (and only) issue of the Peepshow Fanzine is released.

Peepshow HQ, a studio in Bethnal Green is established.

Andrew works on the 3rd series of 'Monkey Dust'.

First Peepshow animation project, 'My Disco is Freezing' for Diesel.

Andrew interviewed at B+A artist management agency. Anthony Andriulli shakes his head as he looks at portfolio, Andrew assumes he's not in with a chance. Surprisingly he is signed.

Andrew & Miles join Black Convoy Illustration collective and go to New York to scout out venues for an exhibition.

Pete leaves INTRO and joins Peepshow – just in time to help Luke on animation duties for the Nike film 'Love The Ball' for Wieden + Kennedy.

2005

Miles is commissioned to create a portrait of Elton John that appears on the side of a fleet of Canadian airplanes.

Jenny illustrates first job for the howies catalogue.

Jenny starts commuting to Cardiff to work on the comeback series of Doctor Who as the graphic designer and propmaker. Continues illustrating between episodes.

Miles' first solo show at Phonica Records, Poland Street, London.

Marie develops the Origarment shoe for Evisu. It sells out from Oki-Ni and wins an international design award.

First Peepshow V&A Fete, leads to stalls in 2005 & 2006.

Elliot & Luke work on the award winning Channel 4 annual report for Browns Design.

New (and award winning) Peepshow website launched, designed and built by Sennep.

Luke exhibits in group show at Stairwell Gallery along with Nick White.

'930sq ft of Peepshow' at Seventeen Gallery, London.

Jenny is commissioned to make a series of 10 book covers. All covers are swiftly ditched and replaced with photographic covers.

Graham Carter, Chris Joscelyne & James Lee Duffy leave Peepshow.

Marie & Chrissie collaborate on a men's fashion story for Complex magazine. Chrissie works with photographer John Short for the first time.

Marie's first solo show at The Lighthouse, Glasgow. Miles and Andrew miss the train and the show.

Miles & Andrew stay in London and visit St Pauls. It's shut.

Andrew & Elliot 'Flyer as Art' exhibition.

Andrew flies out to Singapore to work with MTV Asia.

2006 ∨

Spencer starts a campaign for Zanussi and has to draw feet.

Marie begins an MA in Mixed Media Textiles at the RCA.

Jenny works as a graphic artist and propmaker on the film 'Hot Fuzz'. It's her last freelance job in film/tv art departments.

'Culture Show' title sequence for the BBC.

Andrew's solo show at Recoat Gallery in Glasgow.

2008 ∧

Luke & Elliot begin teaching at Camberwell College of Art.

We take over the windows of Saatchi & Saatchi in Charlotte Street, London for a month.

Recent Brighton graduate Alex Bec joins us at Peepshow.

The first Peepshow Quarterly is produced in an edition of 500.

Our animated sketches for comedy series 'Cowards' are screened on BBC Three.

Form a limited company "Peepshow Collective Ltd'. Miles gets the Managing Director role because his initials are MD.

2007 ∧

Andrew's postcard book 'Of Beasts and Machines' published by Concrete Hermit.

'The Stunt' commissioned by Mesh animation scheme is screened on Channel 4.

Chrissie sets up in a new studio for a month with a team of amazing designers and embarks on the Orange 'I Am' campaign.

Spencer gets a half plot allotment and starts cultivating.

2009 ∨

Luke & Andrew do 'Heavy Pencil' at the ICA. It leads to 'Heavy Pencil East' at Catch, Kingsland Road, London.

Luke takes up residency at Island Fold, Pender Island, Canada.

2010 ∨

Exhibit and run a print workshop at the first Pick Me Up, Somerset House, London.

Andrew's postcard book 'Listen with your Eyes' published by Concrete Hermit.

Elliot starts the 'Inbetweeners' flyers.

2011 ∨

Marie moves to Stockholm. Co-runs 'Detroit', an artist studio space and gallery and becomes senior lecturer in textiles at Beckmans College of Design.

Heavy Pencil events at Pick Me Up 2011, Somerset House.

Luke's first solo exhibition at Krets Gallery in Malmo, Sweden.

Work begins on the Peepshow book with Studio EMMI.

THANK YOU

Peepshow:
Emmi Salonen, Alex Bec, Graham Rawle, Margaret Huber, Peter Nencini, Freya Faulkner, Stephen Lenthall, John Short, Jess Bonham, Fiona Macdonald, Chris Joscelyne, Graham Carter, James Lee Duffy, Robert Grieves, Adrian Johnson, Matthew Hawkins, Gary Powell, Wyld Stallyons, Simon Keep, Nicol Scott, Matt Rice & Hege Aaby at Sennep, Kate Rogers, Nick & Teresa at JaguarShoes, Claire Catterall, Sarah Mann, Lawrence Zeegen, Lydia Fulton, Liz Farrelly, Claire Cook, Kev & Team Rice, Dan, Hayley and Rob at The Mangle, It's Nice That, Ram & all at Quest, All the student helpers over the years.

A huge thank you to everyone at Index Book.

Luke:
Mum, Dad, Dave, Laura, Matt, Rosco, Darryl, Peter, and all at Heart agency – Helen, Darrel, Chloe, Jenny and Amanda.

Jenny:
Pete Davies, Sue Low, Reina Nagakawa, Yuki Maekawa, Dani Golfieri, Amanda Rigby and Anoushka Rodda all of whom have seen fit to commission me more than once. Tim Goodchild, Annie and Clive, all at Kate Spade, Stephanie Pesakoff and Jim Deskevich in the US. An even bigger thank you to Lenny for keeping everything in focus and always bringing me a cup of tea and a biscuit when I'm working late. And thanks to my family and to Ed and Patti for being small and funny.

Miles:
Stephanie Pesakoff and all at Art Department illustration division, Lisa & Rymn at Serlin Associates, Rebecca Sweeting, Charlie Gower, Stephen Lenthall and the 'Tantramar' posse 2002-2006, Paul Pensom & Dan Moscrop, Gareth White for the first commission, Big G & Margaret, Gary Cook, Dani Campbell & Gary Cochran, Chris Ratcliffe and last but not least Rachel Donovan, Jim 'Batman' Donovan for the wealth of reference & Marilyn Donovan for the cheese straws.

Chrissie:
My family and friends, John Short and his team, Stephen Lenthall, Russell Kirby, Alex Plaza, Sarah Kavanagh, Dave Day, Lawrence Seftel, Noel Cottle and all the fantastic folk at Fallon and Orange who made the campaign so much fun to work on, Olivia Gideon Thomson, Anna Kent, Dizzy Downes, Jane Molloy, Alex Bec, Will Hudson, Gavin Lucas, Paul Pensom, James Casey, Kate Rogers, Bryony Birkbeck, Jess Bonham, Lucy Butler, Lauren Davies, Anna Fulmine, Krissy Grundberg, Anna Lomax, Johanna Lundberg, Victoria Shahrokh, Jo Shippen, Hannah Waldron and all the amazing people I've worked with over the years.

Pete:
Kate Dawkins, Chris Sayer, Adrian Johnson, Peepshow artists (past and present), MA Animation course at the Royal College of Art, Adobe After Effects.

Marie:
Thank you to Kristine, Caroline, Eva, Kaspar and Sonay for being beautiful beings and allowing me to dress you up and take your picture. Thank you Rasmus and Joe for your photographic wizardry. Thank you clients and collaborators. Thank you Daniel, my hero. Thank you Mum & Dad for everything. And finally, thank you Andrew, Chrissie, Elliot, Jenny, Lucy, Luke, Miles, Pete and Spencer.

Andrew:
Martin Bundock, Matt Lisle, Nick and Teresa Jaguar, Mic Graves, Ian McCue, Dave Whyte, Simon Bancroft, Pippa Brown, Harry Thompson, Louisa St Pierre, Matthew LeBaron, Aaron Barr, Fran Rosenfeld, Pamela Esposito, James Casey, Greg Burne, Everyone who's taken part in Heavy Pencil, Transparent Sound, The Marmosets, Jim Stoten, Tom Richards, Stephen Reed and my family.

Elliot:
Derek Yates, Tony Branch, Neil Boorman, Daniel Pemberton, Martin Bell, Sarah Habershon, Adrian Broadway, My family and all the students I have taught.

Lucy:
Graham and Margaret, Stephanie and all at Art Department NYC, Jeffrey Briggs, Danielle, Gary and Fatima at The Telegraph Magazine, Stephen Petch at The Independent Magazine, Mum, Dad, Pete and Tiny Maggie.

Spencer:
Thanks to my dad for giving me the determination to work hard and my mum for adding the balance. Thanks to my sister for the competition and my grandparents who were always so proud.

Thanks to the teachers that pushed and inspired me, and the lecturers that nurtured and directed my strengths. Thanks to the friends I've made along the way and who continue to be my inspiration, and to the colleagues I've worked with, and the clients that allow me to be me. You're all responsible for getting me to where I am today, you know who you are.

Finally thanks to my wife and daughters for the daily smiles and laughter which keep the wheels in place and make my life a happy place to be.

CREDITS

Cover Photography:
Stephen Lenthall

Endpapers:
Marie O'Connor

06–08, 92–93, 129, 168–171:
Photography by Stephen Lenthall
(lenthall.co.uk)

14–17, 56–59, 82–83, 106–109,
174–175, 177, 248–249:
Photography by
John Short (johnshort.com)

18–23, 40–41, 44–45, 52–55,
78–79, 88–89, 96–97, 120–121,
126–127, 139, 181, 184:
Photography by Jess Bonham
(jessbonham.co.uk)

32–33:
Photography by Rasmus Norlander
(rasmusnorlander.se)

60–61:
Interview Illustration by
Andrew Rae

85–87:
Photography by Sylvain Deleu
(sylvaindeleu.com)

124–125:
Detail photography by Guy Archard
(guyarchard.com)

160–161, 223:
Photography by Joe Hutt
(joehutt.com)

Additional text and copy editing
by Fiona Macdonald

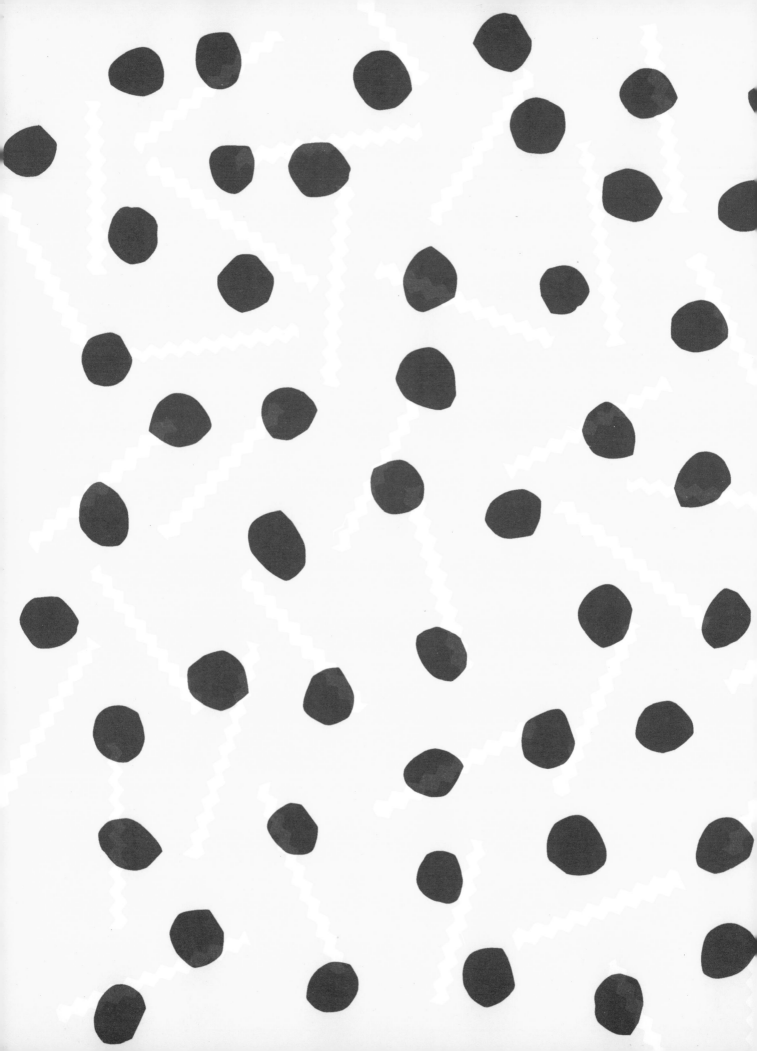